STILL WATERS RUN DEEP

Donald H. Godbold Ph.D.

STILL WATERS RUN DEEP

The Bereolaesque Group

Oakland, CA 94605

Copyright © 2017 by Godbold Family Publishing. First Edition 2017

LIBRARY OF CONGRESS CATALOGING-IN-PUBLICATION DATA has been applied for.

Donald H. Godbold Ph.D.

Still Waters Run Deep: The Blessed Journey of Education, Achievement, Respectability and the Development of Character

Edited by: Enitan O. Bereola, II

Co-edited by: Charlina Allen-Pruitt

Published by: Godbold Family Publishing

ISBN: 0692046283
ISBN: 978-0692046289

Printed in the United States of America

While the author has made every effort to provide accurate Internet addresses and other contact information at the time of publication, neither the publisher nor the author assumes any responsibility for errors or changes that occur after publication. Further, the publisher does not have any control over and does not assume any responsibility for third-party websites and their content. This book is not intended as a substitute for psychological or medical advice. The methods described within this book are the author's personal thoughts. Any use of this information is at your own risk.

Still Waters Run Deep

The Blessed Journey of Education, Achievement, Respectability and the Development of Character

Also by: Donald H. Godbold Ph.D.

A Career in Community College Administration: The Challenges, Successes and Pitfalls of a First African American Chancellor of an Urban Multi-College Community College District

-"If you want it, you can get it." –Godbold

To:

My wife and my children

Dr. and Mrs. Godbold

Godbold Family: Top Back Standing; Dr. Don T.J., Dr. Don H., Christian Godbold, Darwyn Godbold, Aaron Godbold, Andrew Godbold | Middle Row: Dr. Monique T., Michelle Borba, Delores R. Godbold | Kneeling and sitting: Adrien Godbold, Nylah Godbold, Alexander James Godbold, Sarah Michelle Sanchez

Effie Godbold, Dr. Donald TJ Godbold, Michelle Borba, Patricia Cohen, Dr. Monique Toi Godbold Sanchez, Dr. Donald H. Godbold, Dolores R. Godbold

John Jr. and Father John Reilly,
Great Grandmother Delores Godbold and Great Grandfather Donald Godbold,
Great Granddaughters Preslyn and Sienna, Mother Jessica Reilly

Weddng Day: Bridesmaid Sister Ann Cofer, Delores and Donald Godbold, Best Man Timithy Cofer

Wedding Picture: Alice Virginia Kinney sitting down, and Eugene Godbold standing

Jessica Godbold Reilly

Preston   John   Serena

CONTENTS

Preface

There's a story to tell. The effort of this book is to leave an authentic legacy written by me for my children, my grandchildren, my great grandchildren, their propagation, and the Henry Godbold and George Kinney family's genealogy. This book is intended to serve as an incentive and inspiration for anyone, particularly African Americans and other persons of color who may read it, to disbelieve that because of the circumstances of being a so-called "minority," or person of "disadvantage," means that they cannot learn, or are incapable of surmounting the obstacles and impediments that they may encounter in an antithetical world of bias and discrimination.

Introduction

INTRODUCTION

What is known about the genealogy of many legitimate African Americans, whether absolutely true or not, who arrived in the United States of America, as products of the Slave Trade, has generally been passed on by grandparents and older family members for generations by word-of-mouth. I am not ashamed that I am the product, on both sides of my family, of African Americans whose ancestry likely had to survive the horrors and inhumanity of the vicious "middle passage" in being transported to this land by sea while outlasting the atrocities of slavery.

There was a time in the history of slavery when slave plantations had to pay taxes on the number of slaves they had related to the age and sex of the captured. It was not until 1860 that slaves were mentioned by name in the census of the plantation on which they were held. The census also identified them as N (Negro) or M (Mulatto). The term Mulatto (a person of mixed white and black ancestry, especially a person with one white and one black parent), relates to the sexual abuse by slave owners of female slaves that continued even during the period of "Jim Crow" that has been historically well established.

Now watch this.

The Clan

KINNEY CLAN

My nuclear family heritage is from the Kinney and Godbold clans. The genealogy of the Kinney Clan is traceable to a female slave by the name of Grace. Born around April 1830, Grace figures prominently in the Kinney genealogy. Grace married Henry Kinney (sometimes spelled Kenny a Black Slave) around 1850. She had 10 children, five of whom were allegedly by a man named James Meriwether. Mr. Meriwether was probably a White man, who was possibly her slave master. Mr. Meriwether reportedly took some care of the responsibility for the children whom he fathered, but they all carried the surname of Kinney. Grace is my great-great grandmother, and George Kinney Jr., my grandfather, was one of her 10 children.

Follow me.

George Kinney of Eutaw Green, Alabama was born around October 1872 to 1874. George married Annie Pickens, my grandmother, around 1893. The "Pickens" name is the slave name taken by the slaves who were on the Pickens plantation. My grandfather died at his home around the age of 65 after he fell and broke his hip from which he did not recover. I was about 7 or 8 years old at the time. Imagine that. I was present at his home when he passed and was present at his funeral. My grandmother Annie passed around the age of 72 when I was around the age of 16.

All of the Kinney men whom I knew from childhood through adulthood were hard working men. I was told that my grandfather, George, was a coal miner in Flat Top, Alabama. All of my uncles and family men worked in the automobile industry in Detroit, Michigan. Several of them worked in the foundry in order to take the graveyard shift to make the additional pay differential for working those hours. How the family got out of Alabama, I do not know. All of the Kinneys whom I knew had some education, but none of them had finished high school.

Education was important, but the priority was to make a living and to take care of a family. I occasionally had to read his mail to one of my uncles who told me that he was working when he was 9 years old. The job my uncle had was to carry water to the coal miners who worked at the mine where my grandfather also worked as a miner. He was a beloved uncle, an outstanding "outdoors man," a great hunter and a fishing man.

My mother, Alice Virginia Kinney, was a member of the Kinney Clan. I am told that she was an outstanding student and athlete at Detroit's Northeastern High School. She left high school to marry my father when she was in about the 11th grade. My mother, a beautiful and highly intelligent woman beyond her age, greatly valued education and constantly preached that to me, often citing the "Horatio Alger Myth" that was to: learn, try to be the best in everything that you do, excel in school, stay out of trouble and good things will come to you. And don't bring home any bad report cards, or else.

GODBOLD CLAN

Members of the Godbold Clan genealogy can be traced back to a man by the name of Stock or Stockland Godbold, born May of 1837 on one of the three Godbold plantations. The family plantations were established by a man whose name was John V. Godbold. I was told by the Director of Marion County History that John was a seaman who "jumped" ship in South Carolina, and as the first white settler in the area, was instrumental in founding Marion County, South Carolina. Mr. Godbold acquired many acres of land in the county that began the establishment of the Godbold plantations.

John was from Suffolk, England. The Godbold name is well established in Marion County, where there are streets named Godbold and other acknowledgements of the role that the family played in the settlement of the county. The name can be found in many households of Caucasian and Black people throughout South Carolina. Several Black people who live in South Carolina carry the slave name of Godbold.

Stock was married to his first wife, Crissey, in about 1868. They had at least five children, but possibly more. Crissey was about 56 years of age when she died around 1906. Stock is reported to have married his second wife, Lizzie Wilson, about 1905. Lizzie was born around 1886 in South Carolina. There were approximately five children born from this second marriage. My grandfather Henry Godbold was one of the five children.

Not much is known about what Henry did for a living. It has been said that Henry traveled through the South with his family as an "itinerant fruit picker." Henry married Narcissus Fullwood, who lived in Georgia. Narcissus was born about 1887. In this union, seven children were born, four of whom were reported in the Census as Mulatto. My father, Eugene Godbold, was one of Henry's seven children. The circumstances of how that happened are unknown. Henry's oldest children were born in both South Carolina. The others, including my father, were born in Georgia. The journey of how Henry and his family made it to Michigan also remains unreported. The family made it to Pontiac, MI during a time when sugar beets were being harvested and processed for sugar production. Pontiac also had a growing automobile industry and related factory opportunities. It was the automobile industry and employment prospects that later drew the family to Hamtramck, MI and ultimately Detroit.

Education, although considered important was, likewise, not a guiding family force. The men of the Godbold clan were self-oriented visionaries that engaged themselves in more entrepreneurial-type business pursuits. Of the three Godbold uncles whom I knew, I'm aware of one who had a main job in the automobile industry. He also invested in real estate and did quite well. Another beloved uncle was an automobile mechanic who was eventually able to become the owner of his own gas station. The third uncle worked in the haberdashery industry.

My father was a well-built handsome, young man who acquired about the equivalent of a 10th grade education before leaving high school and obtaining a job. I am told that as a young man, he worked in the foundry for the American Radiator Company during the week, making the kind of radiators that were used to heat the homes at that time. He also worked as a barber on weekends. As one of my grandfather's mulatto children, he later used that designation to his advantage and was hired as a Detroit policeman, reportedly the second Black man hired by the Detroit Police Department. At a time when Black men were not being hired by the Detroit Police Department, he added an "o" to the Godbold name to further legitimize not being all Black to get the job. Throughout his adult life he used the surname of Godboldo.

EXHORTATION

My story is a story that many Black men have experienced. It is not unique to me. But this is my story. I hope that it will be appreciated by my nuclear family and others who read it. I also hope that it will be an inspiration for those who doubt their ability to learn, accomplish and put themselves in a position to gain the best of what life has to offer in a climate of despair, disadvantage discouragement, and in many instances, flavored with bias.

"BELIEVE: IF YOU WANT IT, YOU CAN GET IT. TAKE ADVANTAGE OF YOUR OPPORTUNITIES. YOU ARE ABLE. YOU CAN; AND YOU WILL."

Dr. Frank Riesman, a sociologist of note during the Civil Rights Movement, stated that, "The ghettos are America's hidden resource."

He further stated that:

> "The great reservoir of undiscovered and undeveloped intellectual talent in America is not in upper-class or middle-class neighborhoods. While the proportion of high IQs may be lower in underprivileged areas, as now determined, the actual numbers of intellectually very bright children in very poor homes are far in excess of those to be found in the relatively few homes of business and professional leaders."

EUGENE AND ALICE VIRGINIA KINNEY GODBOLD

I was a child of the Great Depression born on October 3, 1928 on the second floor of a house at 13496 Goddard Street in Detroit, Michigan. The home was a few doors down from Peace Baptist Church where my mother and father were married in Northeast Detroit. The house was rented by my mother's sister, Auntie Bessie Mae and her husband, Earl Thomas which during the writing of this book was still being lived in.

My mother and father moved quite a bit thereafter. We lived on several streets in Northeast Detroit bordered by six- and seven-mile roads to the North and South, and Dequindre and Ryan Road to the East and West. The streets we lived on were Gallagher, Charest (on which street the older of my two sisters, Delores – affectionately known as "sister", was born) and 17246 Mitchell Street. I remember the house on Mitchell Street being quarantined because I was sent home after a morning inspection at school that led to me being suspected of having diphtheria, a communicable disease. My father had to enter the home by climbing in through a back bedroom window. Many memories stain those walls. I was circumcised, and had my tonsils and adenoids removed on Mitchell Street.

We eventually moved to an abode at 17169 Mackay Street where the younger of my two sisters, Shirley Ann, was born, and later to another home at 17867 Mackay Street, the last house we lived in before my mother died. The Kinney family always lived close to each other, often within walking distance. Others of the Kinney family also lived on these same streets or shared a house together. Six Mile Road and Jerome Street were parallel to active railroad tracks that transported coal. As children, we had to cross those streets and tracks to get to school. During times of extreme cold, we would go to my grandmother's house near the tracks to share a fire for heat to keep warm. We lived so close to the railroad, my uncles would climb atop the still trains hauling coal and throw it down for us to pick up and put in a bushel basket to take home for fire making.

I am very fortunate that my families moved early on from what was called "black bottom" on the lower east side of Detroit. Black bottom was usually the first location of settlement for new Black arrivals that migrated to Detroit from the South. Black people usually settled there initially before relocating to areas where there was a more concentrated community of other Black families. The area our family moved to from black bottom was a "blue collar" area of factory working men on the outskirts of Detroit where the streets had yet to be paved. There were streets in that area where Black people were not wanted, but there were also minimally integrated streets where Blacks lived without any restrictive covenants that precluded us from living on them. African Americans in those parts lived next door and across the alley from White neighbors. There was a period of time when a White family even lived in the upstairs area of the same house we lived in. A number of my childhood playmates were White.

It must be understood that when I was born, almost from the womb Black youth were told and coached on how to get along with White people; that included learning the extent of how far to go in getting along, and what to do when that extent was reached.

The benefit of living in such an area is that there were a lot of vacant lots or fields on which residents could grow a garden. My mother, other members of my Kinney family and other residents in the community all had gardens as a means of survival where we grew all of the vegetables we needed. One of my chores, of course, was tending the garden.

So it Begins

MY EARLY CHILDHOOD

I was blessed to have been born in Detroit despite its problems of discrimination, segregation and restrictive covenants during much of my childhood and adult life. In spite of the circumstance of race, there were neighborhoods throughout the city that were integrated and Blacks lived peacefully with Whites. Schools in those neighborhoods were also mixed and Black students went to class with White students though there were minor conflicts. However, as was the case at that time, there were many years before the Detroit Public Schools system hired any Black (or Negro as we were called at that time) teachers - an experience in my education that I did not have as a student. I, however, in my assessment as a professional educator, believe that I went to one of the best, if not the best elementary school in the world: Davison Elementary School.

The building was on the corner of Davison Avenue and Joseph Campau Street. We lived quite a distance from the school when we moved to the house on Mackay Street and had a long route at an early age. My mother, however, was keen to realize the value of attending an institution that was well integrated at the time. She enrolled me in kindergarten in September, a month before I turned 5 years old. During this era, schools had mid-year promotions. For example, the first half of the school year for a student in the 4th grade was called 4B. We took "Inventory Tests" at each grade level and students who did well on their Inventory Tests advanced to the next level, or grade 4A, for the second half of the school year. The students who did not do well during a half semester before summer vacation could make it up by going to summer school. At that time, students began kindergarten for a half-day in the morning during the first half of the school year, and for a half day in the afternoon during the second half of the school year. Drop-offs were a challenge. I must admit I was wildly attached to my mother and a bit of a crybaby when I first started kindergarten, but soon learned to enjoy school due to two of the best and most unforgettable teachers, Ms. Dorothy and Ms. Marie. They were absolutely wonderful.

ELEMENTARY SCHOOL

Davison Elementary School was on the border of one of the two other cities within the city limits of Detroit. The city was Hamtramck and was known as one of the most densely populated cities of Polish-speaking people and culture outside of Poland. Hamtramck attracted many immigrants from Poland who lived within the Detroit area, but at the borderline of the two cities. The school also attracted children of families from other Eastern European countries and nationalities such as Russia, Czechoslovakia, Serbia, Yugoslavia, Greece, Turkey and other countries in addition to African Americans who migrated from the American South to the cities North. Many of the foreign students were of the second generation in their families. They not only had to learn American education and fluency of the English language, but also social and cultural behavioral elements of living in America. Our Davison Elementary schoolteachers were like missionaries bringing a message to children who needed to get a decent education and learn good health practices and habits along with receiving the individual nurturing necessary to become great American citizens.

My elementary school days were at a time before there were vaccinations for many of the well-known communicable diseases to avoid against their spreading amongst school children and the community. Before classes began each morning, students lined up close the classroom windows row by row. The teacher's inspection consisted of a spatula to examine the mouths and throats of students, looking for any noticeable infection. They also examined the heads and necks of students for impetigo, "tedder, or ringworm," and lice.

If any of these kinds of infections were noticed, the school nurse was notified. The nurse would then notify the public health department and the student would be taken home. If necessary, their home would be quarantined.

The inspection was absolutely necessary for all students because personal hygiene was very important considering so many nationalities and cultures that were represented at the school. I remember the teachers presenting lessons teaching students about the need to have and use their own wash rag at home, brush their teeth every day, and how to keep their hair clean in order to prevent lice. There were students with long hair who came to school with their hair noticeably cut short because of lice.

HOMEROOM

Davison Elementary School went up to grade seven. We had "homeroom" and "special classes." After we moved from what was called primary grades to grammar grades, we spent half of the day in homeroom and the other half "platooning" to special classes.

Homeroom subjects consisted of:

Reading: It was a time when we read about the milkman who had to get up early in the morning to care for his horse and get him ready for delivering the milk. Sometimes when the milkman made a drop near school at noon recess, he would let some school kids ride on the milk wagon with him and help him make deliveries. Students also had to read about "Little Black Sambo." The story reading of Little Black Sambo was allowed at that time. It was a fable about a Black boy and experiences he had that were extremely stereotyped in depicting the situation and circumstances of a Black boy.

Spelling: We had spelling books and were taught a different lesson every week. We had to learn how to spell new words, use them in a sentence and prove our aptitude on a weekly written spelling test. We occasionally had oral drills at the end of a spelling unit as well.

Handwriting: We had to learn cursive and solid penmanship using a pen with a detachable metal point used to dip in ink. It was fun to watch the janitor come in and fill the inkwells on our desk, but we were penalized if we made a blot on our paper.

Social Studies: Social Studies was a combination of both national and international information. We studied about the geography and culture of other countries as well as our own - including our political foundation. This was usually taught by special material other than our regular reading books.

Arithmetic: Arithmetic consisted of the fundamentals of addition, division, subtraction, fractions and exercises using story problems and measurements like inches, feet, yards, dry measures of pints, pecks, bushels, wet measures of pints, quarts and gallons.

I can vividly remember a few of my favorite homeroom teachers – two of whom in particular taught reading and handwriting.

They were outstanding teachers. Years later when I was a Detroit schoolteacher, one of the two was a substitute at the school where I taught. I believe she remembered me. My handwriting teacher was a good, but strict teacher who taught penmanship and commanded quintessential cursive handwriting. She tolerated no misbehavior in her class.

SPECIAL CLASSES

Music: We went to music primarily to sing and learn historically classic songs of the south, patriotic songs about America and a few selective popular songs of my elementary school years. Included amongst those songs were Negro spirituals. Our music teacher also developed a Davison School Choir for special programs. I enjoyed the class, but was not much of a singer. I met my music teacher again years later when I had been promoted to an administrative position at a Detroit junior high school. He had advanced to a supervisory position in the Detroit Public Schools music hierarchy, and was at my school on a supervisory mission for our music department.

Literature: Here, we had to select a book to read, handwrite a three-page report about it and make a presentation to class. We were taught how to develop an outline, organize the report, use paragraph structure, select sentence structure, the proper parts of speech and present quotations.

Library: In our library class, we learned the value of reading, which led me to an appreciation of books. You could not download an ebook in my days. We had to learn how to go to the public library to select books and care for them as well as understand how to put items in alphabetical order. If you are privileged enough to remember Dewey Decimal system, then you know what I am talking about. Today, we use the Library of Congress to classify books. In my youth, we were urged to use public libraries. I still remember our librarian, who had us learn the alphabet backward and tested us on it. I became a voracious reader and read all of "The Doctor Dolittle" series, "Gulliver's Travels," all of the "Don Strong" series, "Daniel Boone," "Roland and the Knights of the Round Table", "Tom Sawyer", "Huckleberry Finn" and others. I became such a reader that there were times my mother caught me reading by flashlight at night in bed. We, unfortunately with such an Anglicized education, were not made aware of many books to read about Black people or Black history at that time. The stories of Black people were left off of the reading list almost all the way through my public school education except for the mention of Black people who gained some notoriety for doing something outstanding.

Shop: Students in shop class learned to use the tools of the time: the coping saw, plane, file, ruler, yardstick, sandpaper, desk vice, hammer, different saws, screwdrivers, chisels, and shop safety amongst other shop tools. We were taught how to make and repair home necessities, such as window sticks; how to install wall plugs; make and repair table lamps; fix and install broken windows; unclog drains; make magnets; and build birdhouses, amongst other shop projects and assignments.

Auditorium: Symphonic music was played in order to learn how to appreciate that particular kind of music. The teacher narrated what the musical instruments were supposed to be conveying in each song. Students had to be quiet and learn how to be a good audience as well as sit in auditorium seats. Every year we were asked to bring a small amount of money, seven cents or so, to pay for a bus to take classes to hear the Detroit Symphony play. We would put on skits, or small plays, and tried to be comedians, sing or recite poems. The piano, violin and accordion were quite popular. We were allowed to play whichever instrument we could get a sound out of. I believe the intent of auditorium was not only to teach spectator and audience skills, but to also allow students the opportunity to nourish and display some of our entertainment talent under the direction of an instructor.

Gym: In hindsight, gym was a fantastic class. We not only had our regular physical activities and games, we also had to learn multicultural activities, such as ballroom dancing and the dances of the other nationalities, especially the Polish Polka. At the time the Detroit Public Schools had a citywide athletic program called "The Junior Olympics" that was implemented shortly after school began in the fall of the school year. The program consisted of baseball throw, a dash, sit-ups and push-ups, rope climbing, broad jumps, hop skip and jump, and possibly something else I've forgotten. I always enjoyed gym activity and sports. I competed in the Junior Olympics

26

during the beginning of 6th grade and was fortunate to win a silver medal. I participated again when starting the 7th grade. I had practiced the events and won a gold medal that year. I was so proud of myself that I kept those medals for about 77 years, and recently gave them to the older of my two sons to keep and pass on. I was very proud. They were my major accomplishments in an athletic career.

Showers: There was a class called showers that we as boys had to take. I don't know about the girls. The boys went to a room in the school that was equipped for taking a shower. We unclothed ourselves and went up some steps to the shower room. The person who turned on the water, I believe, was a janitor. We soaped up and were given some fun shower activities of how to properly bathe ourselves while the shower teacher alternately changed the temperature of the water from warm to cold on us. After you became wet, it was fun.

DENTAL HEALTH

I do not know if Davison Elementary School was unique in this respect, but the school had a well-equipped dental office. Students who noticeably needed dental work during morning inspection were sent to the dental office. I saw students whose teeth were totally black go to the school dentist and had beautiful white teeth the next time I saw them. Of course, the dentist also filled and pulled teeth. I don't know or have heard of any other elementary school that had a dental office in the school.

The diversity of Davison Elementary School was prominent. Every other year that I was a student there, the school had a Demonstration Week where students of the different nationalities would demonstrate their culture for the community - including, but not limited to dances, music and national way of dressing. This went on for the whole week with certain days for the various nations. The participation of African

American students included dressing in white robes and singing spirituals, as well as performing with White students in the school choir and demonstrations of some of the dances that were taught during gym class. All of this may have been unique to Davison Elementary School because of its location. It was a good time and quite educational for all.

DAVISON ELEMENTARY OPEN WINDOW SCHOOL

On the same grounds as a part of the Davison Elementary School was an "open window" school for children who had health conditions or who had been hospitalized and needed special attention because of their health. Students who were assigned to this school had a naptime during the school day and were fed nourishing food and snacks in addition to being taught their school subjects. The younger of my two sisters, Shirley, was placed in this school after being in a sanitarium for almost three years from the age of six.

JACOBY SPECIAL EDUCATION

Jacoby School was also a school on the grounds of Davison Elementary School. It was a special education school for what was then called "slow learners." It was a great school used for teacher training of students majoring in special education. It was one of the schools where I was assigned for training when I was being taught to be a Special Education teacher, which was my undergraduate major.

It should be fairly obvious that during those years of my elementary school education, I, in hindsight, think so highly of Davison Elementary School and the education I received.

I experienced my first broken heart while attending Davison Elementary School. I was called out of class more than once to take my beloved pet dog, Wimpy, home because he had followed me to school. Wimpy was always the first to greet me when I got home. I got home one day and was not met by Wimpy. When I asked where

28

he was, my mother very sadly told me that he had been hit by a car, and unlike what she had done previously for other similar incidents, she did not think she could nurse him back to health again and had to have him put down. I was heartbroken.

17867

17867 MACKAY STREET

I was the eldest of three children and the only male. My mother was a wonderful stay-at-home wife and mom. Childhood was very conventional and well supervised due to strict discipline.

The last house that we all lived in together as a family did not have a garage or grass in the backyard. The street was unpaved. A truck would come by and spray the street with oil so that the dust would not blow into the homes. We still lived there when the streets were paved by workers in the Works Progress Administration (WPA).

My sisters and I played in the backyard in the early part of the day. We were not allowed to leave the backyard until afternoon to play in front of our house and sit on the front porch until we had our midday bath and had put on clean clothes. On Sunday mornings, my mother would grease my legs when I wore short pants and dress my sister, Delores, and me for Sunday school and church. On the way to church, we would have to stop by the home of my mother's sister Annie Lou's (affectionately known as "Auntie") to get my sister's hair done before continuing on to church.

HOUSE CHORES AND FUN TIME

I loved school. My mother wanted nothing but perfection. She always reminded me that I was in competition with other students in my class to be the best. I also had household responsibilities and chores. I was about 10 years old when I had to scrub the bathroom and kitchen floors on my knees. If that were not done to my mother's satisfaction, I would not be able to go to the Saturday matinee at the movies. I had to take out the garbage and clean out the garbage can. We did not have any garbage disposals at that time. In the spring I had to weed, water and take care of the garden after I had spade it for planting. I also had to regularly wash our dog, a solid white Spitz that my mother loved, and clean up after her every day. Sister and I alternated weeks for washing the dishes. I also had the added responsibilities of dusting the furniture in my father and mother's bedroom, and making the fire in the furnace to heat our home and keeping it going in the winter.

I loved playing outdoors. My love of baseball led me to keep the box score of the games, organize my own neighborhood baseball team, and actually remake baseballs by sewing the covers for out-seam and in-seam baseballs. My playmates and I also had a "scrap up" football team. We played tackle football against other neighborhood blocks using towels for shoulder pads.

In the fall after the gardens were harvested and there were still some tomatoes left in the fields, my playmates and I would often end the season with tomato fights. We got plenty dirty and smelly, but it was fun. My playmates and I also enjoyed digging a hole in a vacant lot, building a fire in it and roasting a potato to eat. We never had a problem.

As kids in the neighborhood, we would build a small wall around the four sides of a vacant field as snow covered autumn leaves and fall changed to winter. The Detroit Fire Department would flood those fields for us to use as ice skating rinks. My mother bought me ice skates and a sled. I became a fairly good ice skater. I also loved to flop on my sled. I loved to lie on my sled on late winter evenings under the corner street light, and watch snowflakes fall. These were thoughtful and reflective moments by myself on Mackay Street. There were not many cars on the roads at that time in my neighborhood.

A notice was put out that there would be a summer instrumental music class offered at Cleveland Intermediate School located a long distance from where we lived. I was interested in playing a musical instrument. I convinced my mother to let me go the long distance for the class where I began to learn how to play the clarinet courtesy of my teacher, Mr. King.

GRANDMOTHER KINNEY

It happened during one summer that my grandmother, my mother's mother, known to us as Grandmamma, and who was the mother of our church, had a stroke while testifying at a Sunday church meeting. Though she was well known at the church, no one knew exactly where she lived. They did know, where her son–in-law, a policeman, lived. Hospitals in Detroit at that time were not that hospitable toward Black people and there was no 911. Grandmamma was brought to the house where we lived. My mother and father were not home. I was home alone. Grandmamma was put in my parent's bed and left there. That proved very inconvenient for us because we only had a five-room house with two bedrooms.

My dad took it all in stride and adapted to the situation. Detroit policemen at the time worked three shifts: days, afternoons and midnights. My dad was able to adjust his sleep needs according to the shift he was on. My mother did likewise, but of course got the day and night lion's share of caring for my grandmother with a great deal of disruptive sleep. I was given the job of sitting by the side of Grandmama's bed to keep her from trying to get out of bed.

Grandmamma was eventually taken to her home where she lived with Auntie. I am pleased that Grandmamma recovered from the stroke and lived for a number of years to become an integral factor in my life.

MY FATHER, A CAUSE OF MIXED EMOTIONS

I was always proud of my father because he was a good and respected policeman. I know that he loved his children. Dad was always good to us and put us to bed at night when he was at home.

We had a going-to-bed ritual that he established, which was putting some jelly on a couple of Ritz Crackers, and we looked forward to having them before going to bed. Dad loved the movies and took my sister and me to the movies, even if we had to walk. The movies changed two or three times a week at that time, dependent on the picture. During the summer, he took me swimming at Belle Isle, a well-known Detroit Park and often along with him to visit men friends of his. He was always home and never an "absentee father." At a time when fowl was bought alive, he would kill and clean the chicken and turkey for dinner and holidays.

My dad, however, was a source of mixed emotions for me. I loved my mother dearly, but my dad was a source of consternation and pain for her and unsettled sentiments for me being that he was a policeman. He was very irresponsible with money; his car was repossessed; and he did not buy a home until I was out of college and in the Army, among other irresponsible embarrassments over the years. This should not have been the case, especially during the years of the Depression when he was not only working, but had a good job. We always had money problems that raised the question of why? My mother questioned his getting dressed up in a dress suit and his dark blue shirt, white tie, white hat, and spats to go to work in the early evening for a duty that was called "clean up" during the Prohibition years. Clean up meant being dressed to be able to get into speakeasies and after-hours clubs to raid them for selling whiskey. I still have some of his files from the raids. The outfit was the uniform for the evening. My mother questioned that, especially when he would come home in the late morning claiming to have been in court. This created a very tempestuous relationship between my parents that often became physical. There were times when I was awakened at night and had to stand between them to keep them from fighting. Neither I nor my mother's side of the family liked the physical abuse received by my mother, and that formed a hatred toward my dad by them and the ambivalence I had for him.

34

The rule in our family, which was the same in the culture of many Black families raising children was, "To spare the rod was to spoil the child." For us, to get what we called a "whipping," usually with a belt or switch on the legs that any adult in the family, particularly Grandmamma, could use to punish a child for disobedience or other disrespects was considered a constructive or positive act of raising a child to be a better person growing up. A whipping was never a beating, but it did sting and conveyed a punishment for your wrongdoing.

MOTHER'S HOSPITALIZATION

It so happened that my mother had to leave our house for a short while. I was told specifically not to go across the street to play in the field, a vacant lot used as a baseball field, because it had rained and the field would be muddy and she didn't want me tracking it back into the house. I disobeyed her and went across the street to the field. My mother came back home sooner than I had expected and caught me in the field. I was punished and received a whipping. I could tell something was wrong with my mother because I could feel the strap, but it didn't sting or hurt as much as usual. I pretended that I was hurt and cried to please her to make her feel that I had been duly punished for my disobedience. I knew that my mother was not feeling well, but I did not know the extent of her illness.

This incident took place not long before my 12th birthday. My mother knew I wanted to be a Boy Scout. The Scout Troop I wanted to join was some distance away at Peace Baptist Church near Davison Avenue. Shortly after I turned 12 years old on October 3, my mother told me that I could join the Boy Scout Troop. It was unusual that two of my aunts, my mother's sisters, were at my house on the evening that I was to go to join the Troop, but I was not sensitive or curious enough about why they were there to ask any questions. I went to the Boy Scout meeting and joyfully came home later to tell my mother all about the meeting, as I usually did when I came home from school. I was informed by one of my aunts that my mother was very sick and had been taken to the hospital. It suddenly dawned on me about why they were there and what had taken place. I was first saddened and then angry about why I had not been told that my mother was ill enough to have been taken to the hospital. This was my second heartbreak. My aunts knew how attached I was to my mother, what she meant to me and how much I loved her. That was the last time I saw my mother up close to talk to her. She had been committed to the Herman Kiefer Hospital. I could not go into the hospital to see my mother, but I could see her and try to talk to her from her hospital window. She always asked about our pet dog, Spot. She elicited from her sister, Annie Lou, "Auntie," the commitment to see that her children, Donald, Delores and Shirley would be cared for. My mother died in February 1941, four months after entering the hospital at the age of 29. She died from Tuberculosis (TB), a very communicable disease at that time. TB was raging. I had two cousins who were also admitted to Herman Kiefer Hospital and two intermediate high school classmates who were also hospitalized during that period. One of the two classmates died. It was known by her family that she thought a lot of me. I was asked to be a pallbearer at her funeral.

Black funeral homes were very few at that time. Embalming and preparing a body for a funeral and burial was usually down in an undertaker's laboratory, so to speak, in facilities that were arranged for that kind of business in their homes. Bodies were usually laid "in state" at the home of a family relative, as was my mother's at Auntie's house. A purple wreath was posted on the front of the outside of the house so that neighbors and people walking up and down the street would know that a death had occurred at that house and a body was inside. The wreath also served as a sign for people to have respect for the dead and the families in the house. Anyone passing by the house or neighbors was welcome to come in to view the body and speak

36

with the family to express their condolences, which many did, often neighbors and people with whom the family had little contact.

Born Again

A NEW LIFE

There was a hatred that had developed by my Detroit Kinney family toward my dad. The family always believed that the abuse of my mother by my dad broke down her resistance and contributed to her weakness, catching TB and her death. Had the abuse of my mother continued, I might have ended up in a different place than where I am now. I made a vow to myself that I would never hit a woman in anger; a vow that I have kept.

Shirley, the younger of my two sisters who was about 6 years of age at the time had become contagious with a version of TB called Koch's Infection, that could affect almost any tissue in the body, especially the lungs. It was required that she be hospitalized when it was discovered she had the disease. Shirley was admitted to The Florence Crittenden Sanitarian where she was treated for about three years before being discharged at 9 years of age. We went to see her practically every week. We were able to visit her by standing outside of a fence. I am grateful that she was able to overcome the disease. Shirley, by helping the nurses and learning hospital routine while she was a patient, became so impressed with nursing that after high school she went to school and trained to become a Licensed Vocational Nurse (LVN) herself. Sister and I had to be tested for TB every year for years.

AUNTIE AND UNCLE ORA

My dad attempted to maintain a household as a single parent. Sister and I initially had a cousin to take care of us, but that did not work. Because of my dad's work schedule, I had to learn to cook and put some food on the table. I became a pretty good cook. Eventually, it was felt best that my sister and I be placed with our Auntie Annie Lou and her husband Ora Maddox, a wonderful man also affectionately known as Uncle Ora. My father broke up housekeeping and put our furniture in storage. He then lived for a while as a roomer with friends.

Uncle Ora, like I did, loved baseball. At times before my mother died, he would come by our house and take me to see the Motor City Cubs, a Black baseball team, play at a nearby baseball field. Uncle Ora worked in the foundry at one of the Dodge Brothers automobile plants. He was very resourceful. When he was laid off from Dodge Brothers plant for a change of car styles called "change over," he had a pushcart that he used to travel up and down neighborhood alleys. He did this to find saleable items that were being thrown away and could exchanged for money with other men who also traveled the alleys as a business with a horse-drawn cart. Uncle Ora would sell items such as bottles, newspaper and the silver from cigarette wrappers that he had picked up and made into a ball. He also sold Bootleg Whiskey in his basement on Friday and Saturday nights to make ends meet until he went back to work. I got plenty of tennis balls and other items that were not saleable. Auntie also ran a booking house for people who played the numbers, which was illegal at the time.

LIFE WITH UNCLE JOE

Auntie had suffered several miscarriages and was unable to have children. Auntie and Uncle Ora had a house full of relatives living with them. There were Uncle Ora's father, Eddie Kinney; Auntie's and my mother's brother, known affectionately as Uncle Bubba; Grandmamma; Sister; and me. Initially, I slept on the couch till I was given a fold out canvas Army cot that I could put away during the day. I lived there for about four to six weeks before being sent to live with my mother's brother, Maxwell Kinney, also known affectionately as Uncle Joe, and his wife Aunt Annie Mae.

I was in the grade 7A and still attending Davison Elementary School during the time I lived with Uncle Joe. I was what was called a "safety boy" and wore a white belt across my shoulder and waist. Safety boys were stationed at corners to assist students on the way to school to get across the street safely. It was during the latter part of March and early April of 1941 that I began to have difficulty walking and had some pain in my legs, so much so that it was hard for me to get to my corner and to school on time. Being able to get to class was something that I had to do despite the difficulty and pain I was feeling. I was determined because I knew that the safety boys were being given a trip to Navin Field for their duty to see a Detroit Tigers baseball game in April. I loved baseball and wanted to make it to the game. I made it to the game, but could barely climb the stadium steps to my seat. It was shortly after that, that I gave up and truly succumbed to my illness.

My dad was unaware of how sick I was. He picked me up from Uncle Joe's house shortly thereafter and took me to visit a friend. I had become more ill and could not raise my leg to get out of the car. He took me back home to Uncle Joe's house where I became bed-ridden and began to have bed sweats. I perspired so profusely that my bed sheets had to be changed every day. I also had so much pain in my joints and neck that I could not move or walk. My dad arranged for my doctor to see me. Doctors, particular Black doctors, in those days made house calls. Dr. Mack, my doctor, came to see me twice a day for several days and described my ailment as Inflammatory Rheumatism. The medicine I had to take was raw quinine in granular form. I did get much better. I was well cared for by my wonderful Aunt Annie Mae, my Uncle Joe's wife.

I missed school the last of April and all of May and June. Two of my schoolteachers came to my house twice to see me. They informed me that my schoolwork was good and to not worry about graduating. My dad took me to graduation. I remember him carrying me up the stairs to the auditorium. My classmates and teachers were glad to see me. I further received their applause and congratulations when I, unable to go on the stage, was presented the gold medal I had won during the fall semester in the Junior Olympics. I felt very honored and appreciated. I also appreciated my dad for getting me to the graduation. I cannot give Aunt Annie Mae enough credit for what she did for me. This entire ordeal, however, was a bit much for my Uncle Joe, which I understood. Shortly after recuperating, I went back to live with Auntie. My doctor informed me that the ailment had left me with a heart murmur and that I was not to take gym classes. That directive was very serious news for me. My heart broke a third time.

AUNTIE AND UNCLE ORA, SECOND TIME

Going back to live with Auntie and Uncle Ora had been made much more comfortable for Sister and me. More sleeping areas and bed space had become available because Uncle Ora's father had gone to live with another one of his sons and other space arrangements had been made while I lived with Uncle Joe. I began the 8th grade at Cleveland Intermediate School that fall, knowing that I was not supposed to take gym class. I, Instead, took instrumental music. I had learned that the State Fair was hiring young kids to work with the Stevedores to help set up the tents and other simple tasks. The State Fair was quite a distance from Auntie's house where I lived, but I walked the distance and was hired. At the end of the day, I was paid $3.50. It had been a cold day and I was chilly and hungry. At the entrance to the Fair, there was a street car that had been made into a diner. I went into the diner, hopefully to warm up a bit and get something to eat. The owner was very nice. I ordered a bowl of chili. To this day, it was the best bowl of chili that I have ever eaten. It cost me five cents. That bowl of chili was a big help for me in covering the distance that I had to go in order to get back home because the day was becoming even colder That was the first job I ever had to make money. I was thrilled to have earned the cash because I was able to buy all of my school supplies on time without bothering anyone.

West Side

THE WEST SIDE WITH DAD

I was in the first half of 8th grade when my dad remarried. He married Ms. Helen Lightfoot Culp, who had previously been married to a Mr. Culp. Ms. Lightfoot had been the bookkeeper for her brother, Roy Lightfoot, who owned a prosperous well-known Black nightclub called Club B and C, among other Black-owned nightclubs. It was because of the success of his club and his prominence among club entrepreneurs in an area that was called "Paradise Valley," that he was given the title of "Mayor of Paradise Valley." All of the well-known Black entertainers of that time performed at his nightclub.

After marrying Ms. Lightfoot, my dad was transferred from the Davison Station on the far Northeast side of Detroit to the McGraw Police Station on the West Side of Detroit. Once there, he found a beautiful three-bedroom home at 4706 Tireman Avenue. My dad wanted Sister and me to come live on the Westside with him and our new stepmother, so we did. The move was quite an adjustment for us to make because the culture of the home was considerately different. We also had to learn a whole new family. My dad had fortunately bought me a Western Flyer balloon tire bicycle while living with Auntie that played a role in my adjustment to the West Side. In leaving Cleveland Intermediate School, I remember a teacher who knew of my departure and approached me for a big hug. She told me to continue being a good student and that she wished me well.

Shortly after moving to the West Side, I began to learn more about it. We had moved within the boundaries of the more middle class section that was bounded by Grand Boulevard on the East, Warren Avenue on the South, Epworth Street on the West, and Tireman Avenue, the boundary line of where Black folks could live, on the North. I began to realize this when I became the locker partner of a student who questioned how I dressed. I wore a skullcap and lumber jacket or heavy sweater to school. I even wore boots with a scabbard on the side to hold a pocketknife. This was how students dressed where I lived on the far Northeast side of Detroit. I, of course, was viewed as a "country hick." My locker partner informed me that the proper attire for the fall was a topcoat and a cap, not a skullcap. And there was certainly a shortage of babushkas.

I got a paper route that helped me become more acquainted with the West Side where I delivered the Detroit Times Newspaper on my Western Flyer bike to 142 customers for one cent per paper. In addition to the Sunday Times, I also delivered the Sunday Free Press and Detroit News newspapers to customers who wanted to receive all three Sunday papers. I got three cents for each Sunday paper. I also scrubbed floors, washed walls, helped clean people's houses and used my bicycle to get ice for people who had iceboxes. With my earnings, I gave my darling sister school lunch money, and movie show fare with extra money to spend for a treat on Sundays.

McMICHAEL INTERMEDIATE SCHOOL

I started the second half of the 8th grade at McMichael Intermediate School - connected to Northwestern High School. I took band instead of gym, which was a good experience. I wish I had continued band when I started at Northwestern. Marr Elementary School was a third school on the same school site. This was a large school site surrounded by large play fields, baseball diamonds, and tennis courts that were lit in the evenings.

Northwestern High School was a beautiful, magnificent structure with marble halls and stairways. McMichael Intermediate School had once been a Teacher's Education College when teachers only had to have two years of college education to become a teacher.

I completed the 8th grade and was changed to a new homeroom for the 9th grade. The 9th grade was freshman year of high school and was taught at McMichael Intermediate School at the time. My entire school record must have been fairly impressive because I had only been in attendance at McMichael for half of a semester. Black students at that time were "tracked" into the different curricular areas. Most Black students were predominantly tracked into vocational areas: machine shop and drafting for males, and homemaking, commercial and clerical for females, without any parental involvement or further say by anyone. Neither my dad nor my stepmother knew or questioned anything that was taking place at school. My job was to go to school, pass my classes and stay out of trouble. My biological mother, who was very strict on getting good grades and educational achievement, which she drilled into me, would have known and been conscious of the issue of tracking. During freshman year of high school, I was blessed to have been tracked onto the College Preparatory Curriculum. In many of my classes, I was one of two or three Black students in classes of approximately 20 to 25 students. What a blessing that I owe to my mother for having been the force behind me to have always been a good enough student to be tracked onto the College Preparatory Curriculum.

The year was about the end of 1941 and early 1942. These were World War II years. Northwestern High School at the time was emerging from what had been termed a "race riot" that had involved the West Side and much of Detroit. Parents would come to school to get their children from the complex of schools that were on the school site. Northwestern High School was a predominantly White or Caucasian, and mostly Jewish, high school.

Detroit at night was "blacked out." I was still delivering papers and occasionally called to sell "extras" that were distributed about the latest breaking news and recent wartime happenings. Imagine what that was like. The streets were totally dark. We paper boys knew our neighborhood and only went up and down a few close streets where there were houses that we knew. There were no lights showing at all. Those were interesting, but exciting times for everyone – especially a 13-year-old boy. I would yell "extras, extras" and people would call me to buy a paper.

The race riot at Northwestern High School was not felt very much at McMichael Intermediate School where the 9th grade was held except for a few parents coming to take their children out of school. I began the 9th grade excited about having been placed on the College Preparatory track. My courses, as I recall, consisted of the usual English, American History, Geography and other routine courses, as well as Latin and Algebra. I continued to do well academically, especially in Latin, where I received straight A's; it is the language and writing foundation that I use today. I became known by other students in my classes because of my academic ability, to the extent that I was always expected to have the correct answer.

McMICHAEL INTERMEDIATE SCHOOL POLITICS

I became popular enough that two of my classmates who were Caucasian, Sheila Edmiston and Shurly Ash, took me under their wings. I don't know if they were Jewish or not, but I was completely naive about school politics. As we finished the 9th grade and there was to be a class graduation, Sheila and Shurly, with little discussion with me, put my name up for class Vice President. I was elected, and a classmate by the name of George Balch was elected class President. There were to be two graduation sessions on the day of graduation, one in the morning and the other in the afternoon. George and I were both supposed to speak - George in the morning, and I in the afternoon. Everything went well for the morning session. After the morning break and before the afternoon session, George offered to treat me at a neighboring drug store and soda fountain on Dexter

Avenue that was a close walking distance from McMichael before the afternoon session. When we arrived at the drug store, owned by a classmate's family by the name of Fisher, they wouldn't serve me because I was Black, then a Negro. I knew that George's intentions were good. He was embarrassed and apologized to me, and I accepted. I spoke during the afternoon graduation session and it went very well. I was on my way to the Northwestern High School building proper for the next three years.

LIFE WITH DAD AND STEPMOTHER HELEN

My home life, in the meantime, was being disturbed. I had stopped my paper route and got a job working at David Greene's shoe store at 24th and Warren Avenue, making $5 a week. I started doing miscellaneous things, such as taking the clinkers out of the coal stoker, emptying the trash and washing the windows, amongst other things before Sam, the owner, would let me wait on customers; when I began to wait on customers, it was selling baby shoes.

Sister had been left home by herself with a cold. She went to our furnace in the basement with her nightgown on to stoke the fire to get more heat. Flames leaped out of the furnace and caught on to the sleeve of her nightgown. Mercifully, it so happened that our stepmother was entering the house from the back door near the basement from having been at her mother's house who lived down the street. My stepmother, known as "Big Ma," was able to subdue my sister who was running up the stairs on fire. The fire was put out, but my sister was seriously burned, fortunately not on her face or her hair. She was hospitalized for six weeks. Skin had to be grafted from her stomach and transplanted to her underarm and side to heal the wound. Sister was a beautiful young lady. After recovering enough to come home, she called Auntie to come and get her. She left dad's house to live with Auntie and never lived with dad again. Shirley had been discharged from the sanitarium around that time and came home to live with dad and rejoin the family with a stepmother.

We lived at 4706 Tireman Avenue until the house was sold. The new owner wanted the downstairs unit, which is where we lived. This was still during the war years and houses were difficult to find. Men who came to Detroit to work in the factories to produce war equipment and work on different shifts were, in fact, sharing the same bed. We had to move and dad could not find another house for us to move to. Shirley went to live with Auntie.

TWO MOVES

I was placed by my dad and stepmother with a Mr. and Mrs. Holt, people whom I did not know, who lived on Bangor Street on the other side of McGraw Avenue. My dad and stepmother became "roomers" at the home of people who rented rooms; that was popular at the time. The deal was that I was to be able to sleep and use the bathroom facilities at the Holt's house and my stepmother was to bring me my meals each day. I slept on a daybed in their dining room. That arrangement, of course, did not work. I fortunately had my job at David Greene's Shoe Store. With my earnings, I was able to buy a meal and enough to eat when I had a real hunger need. I could buy two breaded pork chops, two sides and bread for 55 cents. I lived with the Holts for about a semester and a half before being rescued by Uncle William, my dad's brother. Uncle William and his wife, Aunt Annie Lee, lived on the East Side of Detroit in Black Bottom, in a four-unit tenement with a coal stove that had a toilet, but no bathroom or bathtub. We bathed in a tin tub. Uncle Leamon, another of my dad's brothers, lived in one of the other units. That was a new experience, but I adapted and liked living with my cousin, William Junior, who was like a brother to me. Junior was a year older than I. We slept together in a twin size bed. I learned how to make it in Black Bottom and enjoyed my stay with loving relatives. I stayed with Uncle William and Aunt Annie Lee for the end of the spring semester and most of the summer before Auntie wanted me to come live with her again. I lived with Auntie until I graduated from high school. During all this time and different living arrangements, I missed only one day of high school and continued to maintain my academic level of scholarship.

Casual Competition

AUNTIE AND UNCLE ORA, THIRD TIME

NORTHWESTERN HIGH SCHOOL BEGINNING ATHLETICISM

When I started the 10th grade, I signed up for instrumental music and the band. I also put myself into a gym class without discussing it with anyone. I did so even though I knew I had been diagnosed with a heart murmur. My gym teacher, Mr. Demery, had us play a game called "mat ball." Students in the class were divided into two groups. Skins and shirts lined up as different sides across the middle of the gym. A ball the size of a soccer or basketball was bounced to go as high as possible in the middle of the gym for either side to get. Then you had to get it to the mat at the end of the gym that was protected by the opposing side, as if to make a touchdown. I happened to get the ball several times and fearlessly muscled my way to the opposing mat, which was noticed by Mr. Demery. After gym class, he approached me and asked if I would like to try out for the high school football team.

I was surprised, but of course I said yes knowing nothing about the football team. As mentioned earlier, I had always wanted to play sports. I felt that this opportunity was a blessing. It began my athletic career for years to come. I was outfitted with a uniform, had the positions explained to me and practiced some drills. It was about two weeks before the end of the season, however, I was encouraged to come out for the team the next season, which I did and traded instrumental music for football. That was not difficult to do since I was using a school instrument and my father was not going to buy me one of my own.

It was after football season when I was watching basketball practice from the indoor track that I saw students jogging around the course.

They were all dressed wearing the same sweat suit. I inquired and was told that they were members of the school track team. I decided to try out. The wonderful Jimmie Russell was the coach. He noticed that I had some talent in the sport, and I became a member of the school track team before the next football season began.

I was living with Auntie on the far Northeast side of Detroit, still working at David Greene's Shoe Store and going to Northwestern High School on the West Side of Detroit. I was never questioned about where I lived because I used my dad's address on the West Side. My typical schedule went like this: leave home early to make an 8:00 a.m. class, do almost all of my homework in my study hall at school, football or track practice from about 2:00 p.m. until 5:00 p.m. and go to David Greene's to work from 6:00 p.m. until 9:00 p.m. or whenever he decided to close. I caught the bus back home to Auntie's house at 9:00 p.m. I was at David Greene's by 9:00 a.m. on Saturday mornings until 10:00 p.m. and back again on Sunday mornings at 9:00 a.m. until 12:00 p.m. The only school work that I did at home was to read for English classes, reading assignments that I had to do at home, or write papers that were required for a class. I had a busy day and week. This was my schedule until I graduated from high school. I did not have time for weekend frivolity and girlfriends. I helped Auntie and Uncle Ora around the house as much as I could during those days, but I was not an expense to them except for a place to stay, some food and clean clothes because of the money that I made at David Greene's.

Whatever arrangements made with them for my sisters and my keep, if any, were between them and my dad. I, however, did keep everyone in good shoes.

I dearly loved Auntie and Uncle Ora. Were it not for them, I don't know where I would be at this time in my life. Living with relatives requires making a significant personal adjustment to the culture of a new environment. There are things that you learn that you can do and should not do.

AUNTIE BESSIE

There was an incident that occurred that brought that last sentence to my realization. We had food to eat, but it was somewhat portioned out. One did not just go into the refrigerator and get anything that he or she wanted. My cousin, the son of Auntie Bessie, who lived not far from Auntie's house, came by one morning while Auntie was away and went into the refrigerator to get an apple. I mentioned to Carl that Auntie would not like him doing that. He took the apple and had some words to say to me. I don't know what he went home and told Auntie Bessie, but she, who was always a family problem and did little for my sisters and me after my mother died, came to Auntie's house and laid me low. She questioned, "who was I to say that Carl could not go into the refrigerator? This was not my house. I didn't own or have anything. I had nothing, and was going to be no good like my no good father." She made Auntie approach me like I had done something wrong; I did not believe I had. This incident of course, dampened our relationship somewhat. I began to realize that I was very much on my own and had to deal with many situations very adroitly and make many of my own decisions.

A blessing I had in living with Auntie was also living with a praying counseling, advising, disciplining and mentoring grandmother as a member of the household. It was Grandmamma who mentored me about being a good person. She made it clear that because I was good in my school work that there was no place for arrogance or running my mouth. She made a statement that I first heard from her and I have always remembered: "Still waters run deep."

She said there was no need to always be running my mouth or having something to say – discounting people because they didn't talk much. I could learn more by listening than always talking, and don't be an educated fool. Grandmamma did not like blues singing. She talked a lot about the "good woman," and educated me about girlfriends. She did not like bright red lipstick and fingernails. She even questioned men sleeping in the same bed with their wives. She thought that sleeping separately would cause a woman to be more desirable for her husband. On many hot and humid summer Detroit nights, when we would be drinking cool lemonade and sitting on the floor at Grandmamma's feet, we would listen to her tell us stories about how Black people were treated in the South by White people and the fate of some of our relatives. I was a great listener and haven't forgotten. She was very pleased when I joined the Community Missionary Baptist Church at the age of 12, shortly after my mother died. Grandmamma was the Matriarch of our family until she died when I was close to 17 years of age. I listened to her and have tried to conduct myself accordingly.

NORTHWESTERN HIGH SCHOOL ATHLETICISM

I did go out for football my second year of high school. At the time, Black students were becoming involved in intramural activities, but were not allowed on the swimming team or golf team; maybe one or two could be on the tennis team and basketball team and in one of the school's choirs. The football team was predominantly White. Players had to have a physical examination before becoming involved in the workouts. The team was examined in the locker room by a doctor. I sat with bated breath as I was being checked out, knowing that I had been diagnosed with a heart murmur and had not spoken with anyone about resuming gym classes, especially about going out for football. I was greatly relieved to pass the doctor's examination. I continued to try out for the team and learned the sport. I had purchased my own football shoes for $5 to wear for practice. I knew I had made the team when Coach Sam Bishop pulled me aside and told me to come to the locker room to get a new pair of football shoes. We played a short punt and single wingback formations. I was a halfback. I became quite good and played in every game.

That same year, I came into my own in track and field. In indoor track, I ran the high and low hurdles, the 220-yard dash and anchored the 880-yard relay team. I wanted to play baseball in the spring when the weather broke and sports were outside. Coach Jimmie Russell suggested that if I wanted to get my varsity letter sweater and stripe for track, I had to run outdoor track. It did not take much convincing because I wanted to wear the red and gray varsity sweater. I ran the same events that I had run in indoor track, with the addition of broad jump. I did well and qualified to run in city track meets. I became a star in both football and track and was elected the captain of the track team.

In the 12th grade, I took over the football team. I became the tail back on the single wing back formation. I called all of the plays and did most of the running and passing, and all of the punting. I was a city standout and highly regarded citywide and on campus, making me feel fully embraced by the West Side. I made the Players All City Football Team, ranking me one of the 11 best football players in all of the public schools in the City of Detroit. I was also the indoor West Side champion in the high and low hurdles and the 220-yard dash. I ran against the East Side Champions in the high hurdles and 220-yard dash for the Indoor City Championship. In each event I took 2nd place. I don't think my father ever saw me play a high school football game, and maybe just one city track meet.

Sheila and Shurly, who had put my name in nomination for class officer in the 9th grade, did so again when graduating from Northwestern High School along with Mary Ann Thornton, a Black student. I was once again elected as the Vice President of my graduating class. Northwestern High School had a graduation ritual of the senior class "passing down the spade." It was a silver spade;

the type used in gardening, with ribbons the colors of all the graduating classes on it. I was honored to have been selected to make the speech to the incoming 12th grade to pass on the spade. I made the speech at a time arranged by the school that happened to be during my English class. The next time I attended the English class, the teacher told me she was dropping my grade from a B to a C because I should have been present in class.

STATUS

I was a "big man" on campus. Well, Ronald Teasely and I. Ronald was a great high school basketball and baseball player. I felt like Northwestern High School and the West Side were my surrogate families. Coming from the far Northeast side of Detroit just to be on the West Side made me well liked and appreciated. I knew that I could stop at my friends' homes including Duke Foster's, Reginald Ernst's and Rowena Wright's, along with a few others, where I did not have to worry about getting food to eat if I was hungry.

I continued doing well in all of my academic studies, getting A's and B's in most all of my classes. I remembered what my grandmother had taught me and did not get excited about the girls who were interested in me until my last year of high school when it was arranged for me to meet a young lady who had been observing me in study hall and wanted to meet me. I was one year ahead of her in school. We got along very well and I started dating her by taking her to football games and later visiting her at her home. She eventually became my high school girlfriend.

I had become noticed by university scouts and was approached by the assistant track coach at the University of Michigan in Ann Arbor. He wanted me to run track only, but no football because of the influx of returning veterans who had either played college ball before the Army or while in it. Competition to make the team would have been steep. I was also approached by Mr. Tom Briscoe, a recruiter from

Western Michigan University. There, I could run track and play football. At the time, there was no scholarship like a "free ride." Families had to contribute to a scholarship such as room and board, travel to and from home and other amenities that my father was not willing to pay. Jimmy Russell and Sam Bishop, my high school coaches, spoke with me and told me that Wayne University was also interested in me. They advised me to go to Wayne University and I accepted their advice. Being admitted was not a problem. I was blessed that arrangements for how my tuition was to be paid had been made with the University's Athletic Department that also included my books. The Athletic Department always made a way for me to make money on campus to pay my tuition, or paid my tuition and fees during all my four years of college.

Even though those arrangements had been made for me, I was convinced by a high school teammate and my best friend to join the Army for 18 months to get the benefits of the GI Bill for going to college. We went to a recruitment station to join on a Monday or Tuesday. My father had to sign for me because I was only 17 years old. We elected to be inducted on the next Monday because my friend wanted to take his girlfriend to the Olympia Stadium to the Paul Robeson concert that Saturday. I went with them. When we went back to the recruitment center the following Monday for induction, we were told that we could not be inducted because the Army had reached its quota of Negroes. I immediately told my friend and myself that if the Army did not want me, I did not want the Army. My friend tried to get me to try other branches of the military. He ended up in the Marine Corps. I went back to Wayne University, tried out for the football team and made the team. I resumed the arrangements that had been made for me by the Athletics Department and began my college career.

College Tales

COLLEGE

Toward the end of high school, I had stopped working at David Greene's Shoe Store. I was asked by my high school Coach Russell if I was interested in a summer job as a counselor at a summer camp for socially maladjusted boys. College students who usually had those jobs were in the Army. I accepted the offer and became a camp counselor during my last years of high school. I met some wonderful Detroit Public School Special Education Teachers. The introductions sparked my interest in majoring in Special Education, which was my undergraduate major in college.

I quickly found that going to college was quite different than going to high school. Classes and athletic practice were scheduled all day long. Though there was a lot of vacant time on campus, I spent much of it in the library.

Being able to live with Auntie during college was a true blessing. There were, however, some difficult days. I no longer had the small change in my pocket that I earned from working at David Greene's Shoe Store and had to get to midtown to go to college. Bus fare was 10 cents and streetcars were seven cents. Pennies in those days were valuable. I did not get any money from my dad, who lived some distance away on the West Side. I do not remember Auntie or anyone in the household ever giving me carfare to get to college. Still, I never missed classes.

Several times I would get up early in the morning and go up and down the neighborhood alleys searching for milk and soda pop bottles that I could redeem for money at the local grocery store to get enough carfare money to get to college. I did not worry about getting back home. There was always a way. A good friend of mine who worked for the Department of Streets and Railways (DSR) three hours a night cleaning the buses knew of my transportation need. He told me that in cleaning the buses he could get me transfers that had been used, but were still good. He said that he would show me how to use them for bus and streetcar fare for those lines that crossed each other. That solved my transportation problem for my last years of college when needed.

NO MONEY, MORE PROBLEMS

I was met with another problem while attending Wayne University that had become a State University. Even though the Athletics Department always saw to it that I had a job on campus, those jobs were for me to use to pay my tuition and fees that totaled $75 per semester. When I got my paycheck, I religiously went to the Bursar's Office and paid on my tuition. There was one occasion in the spring of the year when the winter snow and ice was melting and I had holes in my shoes; stuffing padded paper around the insoles did not keep the water out. I took the money that was to be used to pay my tuition and bought a pair of inexpensive shoes. I missed my payment to the Bursar's Office. When I went to my classes, I was told by my instructors that I was not allowed to attend, sometimes abruptly in front of the class, or politely outside of class in the hall. I was literally put out of school until I settled the debt. I did not want the Athletics Department to know about what happened. Fortunately this happened between athletic seasons. I did not know what to do because I did not believe that I would get any help from my dad or home. I went back to Northwestern High School and explained to Coach Russell what happened. He did not question me about whether I wanted to stay in college or not. He simply took out a piece of paper, wrote a name on it and told me to take it to the Chrysler Motor Car Factory that was located on East Jefferson near the Belle Isle Bridge and give it to the man whose name was on the paper. I did that. The man without hesitation gave me a job on the Chrysler assembly line. I worked there for a week and made more money than I had ever made in my life. I found out later that the man whose name was on the paper was Coach Russell's father. I quit the job at Chryslers, went back to Wayne State, paid the Bursar's Office and resumed my classes. It was as though I had never missed a class. I ended the semester with good grades. It was the only time I ever faced that problem again. The Athletics Department eventually paid all of my tuition and fees until I graduated.

LOVE LIFE

I resumed my relationship with my high school sweetheart. We were together for a long time, during which I completed two years of college. I went to church with her on Sunday and ate dinner with her and her family on many early evenings before going to the movies or other dating activities. Her mother liked me very much and could see what my goal was, a college education. I thought that my girlfriend understood my status and what I was trying to accomplish in order to marry her. Her father who worked for the post office gave me an application for a job at the post office and I was ultimately hired. It was in my third year of college. I kept the job from January until July when I received my usual letter from the football coach to prepare to go to our football training camp. I had missed the spring track season. I made the decision to leave the post office and go to football camp to train for the coming season. That decision did not go over very well with my girlfriend's father. I was very naive about girlfriends and women at the time. I thought that I was considered part of the family. When I went to visit my girlfriend one day, I was met by her on the front door steps where she returned a small diamond ring that I had saved for and given to her. She told me that if I did not marry her she was going to start dating other guys. I did not want to work at the post office and I was not in a position to marry her. I did not have the money or family support for a college education. I did not want to lose the opportunity that I had been given to get a college education. I wanted a college education, and if possible, to graduate and attain a professional position. We broke up. She did what she said she would. It was the most serious heartbreak I have ever experienced except the loss of my mother as a young child. That was a different kind of heartbreak.

I continued at Wayne State University. Had I not been so naive about women, I could have probably won her back with some dutiful effort irrespective of her father. My girlfriend's mother still liked me a lot and I knew my ex loved me. When I graduated from college, I made an attempt to get her back, but she told me she had fallen in love with someone else.

Oh well, such is life.

I attracted a lot of girls as a college athlete and did date other girls. I never had to worry about getting food during the school day. There was always some girl friend who had a sandwich or snack for me, particularly a young lady who worked at the student center snack bar. She usually had a treat for me after athletic practices and before my evening classes or on-campus job. She was a former Northwestern High School student who had the "full package." She liked me and looked out for me. She was a professional majorette who was hired to lead parades and bands. She was killed in an automobile accident returning home from a gig in Buffalo, New York.

There were other girls whom I dated, one who had not done well in her first two years of college, but had a city job. She proposed to me and said that we could get married, and she would see me through my last year and a half of college. I would have none of that. So she quit me and married a friend of mine. There were other college girlfriends, some so unofficially attached to me that college men who wanted to take them out would ask me if they could date them. There were none who quite came up to the standard of my high school girlfriend, except one.

ADORATION AND GRADUATION

I made it through Wayne State University and graduated in June of 1950. I had gone to live with my dad briefly during my first year in college for part of a semester when he had an apartment on the West Side. Subsequently, I lived with him during the summer of my last half-year of college when he had finally rented a flat of a two-family flat house on Wreford near the Olympia Stadium. My place of living had been changed nine times before graduating from college and going into the Army, including living with a family that I did not know.

I began working for the Detroit Department of Parks and Recreation full-time as a Playground Recreation Leader during the summer after I graduated from Wayne State University. I kept that job and began teaching as a substitute Special Education Teacher that September. Shortly after starting my professional career, I received my notice and was drafted into the Army for the Korean War in February of '51. I told all of my girlfriends not to wait for me to come home because I did not know if I would come home, or in what condition I might come home. There were two young ladies, however, whom I took seriously as girlfriends at the time. One was two years behind me in college who was not yet willing to commit to a steady relationship, for whatever the future may have held. I wrote her two letters while in the Army. She did not answer either letter - Dear John or whatever. I have not seen her since I left for the Army. In more recent years, one of her sorority sisters told me that she said she loved me. She was a nurse and a very smart person who could have elevated herself to a higher-level job in Public Health. I have seen a name that I knew her by on Death Certificates of my family. My other girlfriend was my last and most serious love before being drafted for the U.S. Army. I did not want to marry going into the Army, and she told me that if I did not marry her she would become a Catholic Nun, which she did. She was a person and a love that I will never forget. I entered the Army girlfriendless.

Be all You Can Be

FORT LEONARD WOOD MISSOURI

When my dad took me for induction, I was vain enough not to want to be turned down because of physical reasons even though I did not want to go to the Army. I was first stationed at Fort Custer in Michigan, and then transported to Fort Leonard Wood, Missouri for basic training. I was placed in an overcrowded all-Black 40th Engineer Petroleum Distribution Company to be trained to keep oil flowing to the battlefront. I went through basic training two times, the second time as a "cadre man." I was asked to teach Troop Information and Education. I became well known within the company. Some sergeants who were called back from World War II who were trying for promotions asked me to tutor them in math. There were other men in the company who knew that I was kind of a straight arrow – the type who did not leave the post on weekends to have a good time in town. Several of them would give me an envelope with money in it and ask me to keep it for them until they returned to post. They would say that they did not want to spend all of their money in town having a good time with the ladies.

PRIVATE TIMOTHY COFER

The company barracks were kept warm by coal-fired furnaces. All of the men in our company became familiar with Timothy Cofer who had been given the duty of keeping the barracks warm. He worked at night. Tim was very industrious and had been trained as an automobile mechanic as well as a barber. Rather than sleep during the day as he could have, he made himself available to do kitchen police (KP) for troopers who did not like that duty that came around periodically. He also did automobile mechanical work for the few troopers who were allowed to have an auto on post.

One weekend when we were practically alone in our company, I came to know Tim very personally. He must have noticed me around the company. I was looking for someone with whom to go to the movies. I happened to go to Tim's barracks. He was sitting at the foot of his bed with one foot locker on top of another writing what looked to be a very long letter. We had quite a conversation before he told me that he did not go to the movies. I even offered to pay his movie fair of 12 cents. He refused. Tim told me that when he went home on his recent furlough he had gotten married and bought a home. I thought that was quite an accomplishment with him being in the Army. I was about to leave him when I made the casual comment that "maybe someday I might meet someone who would want to marry me. Tim said, "Wait a minute. I have nine sisters; there are several about your age who you might like." He spread their pictures out on his bunk and had me look at them. He said, "Pick one you might like. I will recommend you to her and am sure that she will write to you if you write her." Tim's sisters were all attractive ladies. I selected Delores and promised to write her.

Christmas furlough was shortly thereafter. When we returned from furlough, Tim thoroughly chastised me for not keeping my word to write to Delores. I recommitted myself to write to her and that began a six-month courtship by mail. I had only gotten to know her by an exchange of pictures. We wrote at least three letters a week to each other, a task that I enjoyed writing with some pretty good "stuff." I became an even closer friend of Tim to the extent of being called "brother-in-law" by some of the troops who knew of the nature of our friendship. We, with another trooper in our company, Connie Keene, even had Bible Study together.

THE MEETING

I finally went to Washington, D.C. on furlough for about 10 days to meet Delores Roxanna Cofer in June of 1952. The letter writing had been intense. All that we had to do on that visit was meet, personally see and assess each other to determine if each of us was a person with whom we wanted to be. We both passed the test.

The first thing that happened to me on arrival to D.C. after a day-and-a-half train trip was to be taken to church that night. I felt that the good Lord had led me to Delores as the "good woman" about whom my grandmother had often talked. I proposed to Delores on that trip and she accepted my proposal. I asked of her parents if they would approve of our marriage. Delores' parents who knew of our courtship by mail gave us their blessings, with the admonition by her father that after we were married, he did not want to see her come back across his door sill again because of a failed marriage.

I returned to Fort Leonard Wood to complete my tour of duty. We continued our letter writing. I saw Delores for about 22 days at Christmas time. While in D.C., I always stayed at the home of her brother, Curtis Cofer.

FORT LEONARD WOOD HILL TOPPERS FOOTBALL TEAM

During the entire time all of this was taking place, I had gained some good fortune at Fort Leonard Wood. General Perdue, the post Commander, wanted a championship post football team. He put out an order that anyone who wanted to try out for the team could be excused from company duty. I tried out for the team. After about a month of "try out drills," I made the team. My Company Commander offered me a proposition that if I left the football team and took over the supply room, he would guarantee me being promoted to the rank of Sergeant. I informed the football coach about why I was leaving the team and left to take over the company supply room. The Fort Leonard Wood Hill Toppers football team lost their first game.

One day shortly after the loss, I was summoned to the company headquarters "Day Room," and told that the Company Commander wanted to see me. I met with the Commander who told me to report to the post Field House at 1500 and "don't be late." I said, "Sir, I thought that we had a deal." The last words he ever said to me were, "Soldier, obey orders." I, of course was going to obey orders. However, on the way out of the Commander's office, I stopped to ask the Company Top Sergeant about what was going on. He asked me if I had noticed a jeep that came past the supply room into the Company area with a Colonel's insignia on it. I said that I had not. Top told me that a Colonel had been sent from Brigade Headquarters who confronted the Company Commander with the question, "What right did he have to make a deal with Private Godbold to leave the football team to become a Supply Sergeant?" The Colonel ordered the Commander to have me back at the post Field House for the football team immediately, or the Commander would be put on orders to be sent back to Korea. That settled that! I never did have a change in rank, but played two years of football for the Fort Leonard Wood Hill Toppers that lost only three games in two years and was the 5th Army Champions. I was one of five Black players on the team. One of whom, was a player by the name of Jack Crittenden with whom I played in college. Upon leaving the Army, Jack played professionally with the Chicago Cardinals and the Green Bay Packers.

I was transferred out of my Company to an ASU Unit in which the post administrators, entertainers and athletes were located with other post personnel. One of the entertainers was the popular jazz musician, Tommy Flannigan, who also lived on Klinger Street – the same street I lived on in Detroit. It was good duty. I only had to pull KP when nothing was being done related to football, which was about once every six months. I was given an "off duties hours pass" that allowed me to leave the post anytime I wanted to. I could also have street clothes on post and a car if I had one. I was given a good job as a Radio Operator and Controller at the small post air strip to help small Army planes, 126s, 119s and others land, receive service and take off in the day and night. I shared that duty with another soldier. We slept at the airstrip and controlled our time. We agreed that we would work one week on and one week off. I learned a lot about how to do the job. It was a beautiful experience.

I, having been transferred from my line company to the ASU Company, also proved to be very fortuitous for my friend, Tim Cofer, who was to become my brother-in-law. Because of my connections with other members in the ASU Company, particularly athletes, Tim gained some new clients for haircuts and automotive services. Tim trusted me enough to have me to deposit as much as $300 that he had earned in the post bank.

Nothing But Love

PLAN YOUR MARRIAGE BEFORE YOU PLAN YOUR WEDDING

Delores and I planned our wedding - after we planned our marriage, of course. She asked me during our courtship if I, having been raised in the Baptist Church, would join her Church of God Holiness. Although her church was very fundamental, I did. The church was pretty easy to adapt to because its services were much like those of the Baptist Church I belonged to. The church did not have the ritual of a mourner's bench, tarrying, speaking in unknown tongues or other rituals of the Churches of God in Christ (COGIC). The Churches of God Holiness did have a discipline of which members were to obey. If you remember when I was trying to get Tim to go to the post movie with me, he told me he did not go to the movies. There is your example.

TEACHING OPPORTUNITY

I was discharged from the Army in February of 1953. I had gotten an apartment for Delores and me to live in after marrying and coming to Detroit. I had a full-time job waiting for me upon my return from the Army. I, one week to the day after being discharged, was blessed to have been asked to become a long-term substitute at the Moore School for Boys, a Senior Ungraded School for boys 15 to about 20 years of age. The regular teacher had been in an automobile accident in which a passenger was killed and the teacher himself seriously injured. I was fortunate to have worked with the assistant principal at the summer camp for Socially Maladjusted Boys who found out that I was being discharged from the Army. Several of the well-known singers of Motown attended the Moore School for Boys; the most notable of whom was Little Willie John, who was quite an entertainer. The offer to teach was a moment of gratitude, and I accepted the position. I had two full-time jobs from February until the end of school in June. This new position took some immediate adjustment on my part. The boys loved their teacher who had been injured in the automobile accident and some of them weren't the least bit interested in education. It was a trying experience. Still, it was a time that I will never forget.

At the beginning of the fall semester, I was transferred from the Moore School For Boys to Sampson Elementary School to teach a Junior Ungraded, "Self-Contained Classroom" for socially maladjusted boys from about the age of about 7 to 15 years of age. I could keep a boy longer who was making good progress to return to the regular grades before sending him to a Senior Ungraded class or school if I wanted to. I remained at Sampson Elementary School until receiving a promotion.

Delores and I were married on Easter Sunday, April 5, 1953, in a beautiful house wedding in front of the fireplace in her home in Washington, D.C. We were married by Bishop T.P. Burrus of the Churches of God Holiness from Atlanta, Georgia. It was a great day for me and I hope for her.

BEGINNING OUR MARRIAGE AND BARTON STREET

Delores left Washington, D.C. and began her married life with me in my hometown of Detroit, Michigan. We were very fortunate that in Detroit there was a Church Of God Holiness, The Mount Moriah Church of God Holiness of the same Reformation as that to which we belonged in Washington, D.C. We first lived in the apartment that I had furnished and decorated for us. We stayed in that apartment for about four months when a friend suggested that I get a loan from The Detroit Teacher's Credit Union (DTCU) and buy my own house. I followed his advice and got a $2,000 loan and bought our first house. It was a five-room bungalow on Barton Street for $10,000 on a Land Contract with a completely finished attic. Our mortgage payment was $90.00 per month. The finished upstairs was rented for $65.00 per month. Our out-of-pocket money for the mortgage payment was $25.00.

We were the first Black people on that block. We were very fortunate. Delores and I began our family. Our first two children, Michelle and Donald T.J. were born while living in that house. We wanted to move from Barton Street after Michelle became five years old so that she would not have to cross Tireman Avenue, a dangerous street, to get to the elementary school she would have to attend. We were fortunate to be able to buy another house and move before she started elementary school.

That house on Barton Street is memorable. Donald T. J. became so ill with the Asiatic Flu around the age of two, that we almost lost him. Taking him to our pediatrician's office was of no avail. He was barely breathing and we believe that he had crawled into his bed and given up to die. Delores and I were also very ill with the flu. We asked for the Saints' prayers of the church. This was on a weekend. We were finally able to contact our pediatrician, Dr. Natalia Tanner, by phone. She heard his breathing and told us to get him to the Detroit Children's Hospital. I wasted no time in getting him there. Student interns and residents were waiting for him and trying to console him when a Dr. Wagner entered the hospital wearing an open neck white shirt and no coat. He picked Donald up, put Don's chest to his ear and said "take him to the operating room." He performed a tracheotomy on Don so that he could breath, but Don was unable to make a sound when he cried. The doctor told me that Don would have been dead within a half hour without that surgery. What a blessing.

My son was in the hospital for 12 days. Delores visited every one of those days to feed him herself. After being discharged from the hospital, he continued with some respiratory ailment that required me

76

to get up at night and take him to the bathroom to run the shower for steam to relieve his breathing. I was talking to the janitor at the school where I was teaching whose son had a similar ailment. The janitor recommended that we see his doctor. We took his advice and made an appointment. The doctor prescribed some medicine that our pharmacist had to send away to get. The medicine prescribed cured Don's respiratory ailment. I feel pleased and blessed that the medicine was effective and Don had a successful recovery from the ailment.

It is remorseful to have to report that the couple who bought our house on Barton Street lost a son who was killed by an automobile while he was crossing Tireman Avenue, the same street that we did not want our daughter Michelle to have to cross to get to the elementary school she would have to attend if we had continued living on Barton Street.

GRADUATE STUDY AND MARRIED LIFE

I began to take full advantage of the GI Bill and returned to Wayne State University to earn a Master of Education Degree in Counseling (M.Ed.). The GI Bill was not only helpful in attaining the M.Ed., I also received $80 a month for going to school; that was a great financial help. Detroit teachers were paid for 10 months at that time. We were not paid during the summer or for the weeks of Easter and Christmas holidays. I took postgraduate courses after earning the M.Ed. to also earn an Educational Specialist Certificate that added a bit more to my paycheck. I was still working weekends as the Center Director at the Kronk Community Center for the Detroit Department of Parks and Recreation, which essentially was three jobs with several different responsibilities. I became a member of the Varsity Club Incorporated Organization of Former College Athletic Letter Winners who had won a varsity award in a college sport. A member of that club known as Tubby Washington, who was also a

Plant Superintendent for the Ford Motor Car Company, got me a job one summer in the foundry at the Ford Rouge Plant. Most teachers at the time usually had to find summer work. I worked in the foundry for several weeks as a core handler and on the shake out. Both of these jobs were handling hot steel that had gone through a furnace. We wore gloves and had the proper safety equipment. One day as a core handler, my hand slipped and I braced one of the cores with my chest. The heat burned through my T-shirt and across my chest.

In the foundry, you had to search for your lunch because it was covered with dust. When I'd go home, my wife would make me take off my clothes at the front door as they were filled with dust and dirt. The night I came home with the burned skin on my chest because of my mistake, Delores said, "That is enough; no more foundry." That was the end of the Ford Rouge foundry for me.

I decided to take the necessary courses for certification to teach Adult Education and again returned to Wayne State University. I thought that teaching Adult Education would be more related to my day teaching job and allow me to only have to moonlight two days a week. It was a good move.

THE DETROIT MOVE FURTHER WEST

We bought the house of a Rabbi in a Jewish neighborhood and moved from Barton Street to Cortland Street between Dexter Avenue and Holmur. After we had moved into the new house, the Rabbi asked us if his mother could come to our house on the Sabbath Day to wait to be picked up to go to the nearby Synagogue. Of course we said yes. She had a seat in our bay window. That went on for several weeks.

Once again, we were the first Black family on the block. Michelle was able to easily walk safely to Winterhaulter, a wonderful neighborhood elementary school. The younger of my two daughters, Monique Toi, was born while we lived on Cortland. We enjoyed our life there and made many friends as more Black people began to become neighbors on the block. Our best friends were Rufus and Atha Powell who lived across the street from us and whose daughters from time to time babysat for us. Rufus got us involved in going "smelt" fishing, which we enjoyed. We also became well-acquainted with our next-door neighbors, David and Armine Cason.

After a while, Delores and I decided that we needed to move further West for better schools. We left Cortland Street, however, we continued our association with all of the friends there.

We bought a house on Santa Barbara, one block from 7 Mile Road, again in a Jewish neighborhood. Michelle began Hampton Intermediate School, one of the highest socioeconomically ranked intermediate schools in Detroit. Donald Terrence attended Bagley Elementary School. The younger of my two sons, Darwyn Eugene, was born while we lived on Santa Barbara. We were once again the first Black family on the block when that area began to sell homes to Black people. We gained some very nice neighbors, one of whom was Rabbi Leonard Cahan. We are lifelong friends even still at the time of this writing. Michelle would spend the Sabbath Day and night at the Rabbi's house with his children. Darwyn attended day school at the Jewish Synagogue. Our family was invited to share the Jewish holiday festivities with the Cahans' and activities at the Synagogue.

MOUNT MORIAH CHURCH OF GOD HOLINESS

Delores and I were regular and faithful members of the Mount Moriah Church of God Holiness where our children also became members and were baptized. Some of the most wonderful people whom I have ever gotten to know were members of the church and also became good friends and loving Godparents to our children. Our children attended church regularly and not only became knowledgeable about church discipline, but also gained a respect for the religion. As Christians, they learned to respect elders and other people with whom they came in contact.

Delores and I had to reconcile some of the cultural differences on how we were raised. I particularly wanted our children to have a conventional childhood life. I did not want my children to be considered unconventional or odd by other children with whom they would be going to school and playing because of our religion. Delores and I agreed to compromise, and with discretion, let them enjoy many of the same things that other children enjoyed. We took them to special children's movies, such as "The Song of The South," "Zippety Do Da," and others. We let them enjoy popular music and they never missed a Motown Review at one of our Detroit downtown theatres, or Red Rocks Concerts when we lived in Denver after we left Detroit. I am proud of the adults they have become.

Educated Black Man

PROFESSIONAL PROMOTIONS

My fortunes began to rise with the Detroit Board of Education. The Board at the time would announce administrative position openings and the extent of the list of names for the position they were going to establish. For example: a list of 50 names for the position from which to choose for promotion when a position became available. The selection process to make the list involved a written examination and an oral interview. An applicant had to score high enough on the written test to earn an oral interview. I applied to take the test for a Counseling Administrative position and successfully met the requirements of the process.

I was selected to be a counselor at Burroughs Intermediate School of the 7th, 8th and 9th grades on the mostly White Polish Catholic East Side of Detroit near VanDyke Avenue. The Burroughs Intermediate School Attendance District included a neighborhood that was fast gaining a sizeable Black population that was separated by an expressway. There was a bridge that students from that neighborhood would have to use to get over the expressway to get to school. The school was in a racial transition. There were only three or four other Black teachers and I was the first Black administrator. There were three counselors. We each followed a grade through graduation. I started with the 7th grade. Being the first Black administrator, I knew it was going to be a challenge. There were White teachers who would not send their students to me for counseling. When I had to discipline a White student who had to be sent home, I was not surprised to be called on the phone by an irate parent or sibling who did not mind using the "N" word. Administrators at the school were also asked to arrive at school early to patrol near the expressway in the event of fights that might take place with the Black students who came across the bridge to get to school. I also had some differences with the Principal, Mr. Brownell, who had succeeded the principal who was there when I arrived. He did not quite know how to relate to another administrator who was Black.

DOCTORAL INTEREST

While studying for my M.Ed., I was impressed by the jubilation expressed by my psychology professor and classmates. He announced that he had met all of the requirements for his doctorate degree and could now be called Doctor. I did not know that a person could be a professor teaching a university class like psychology without a doctor's degree. I was not knowledgeable about graduate assistants teaching classes. It was that particular incident that caused me to start thinking about earning a doctorate degree since I had earned everything else in education offered at Wayne State that was meaningful to me in my employment by the Detroit Public School System. That incident, as simple as it was, caused me to speculate and begin to research the possibility of earning a doctorate degree since I still had a considerable amount of the GI Bill left that I could use. It was something that I knew I could do if given the opportunity.

I first inquired about doctoral study at Wayne State, but found out that the university was not necessarily hospitable to local Black students who wanted to pursue a doctorate degree. We noticed, however, that Wayne State was hospitable to Black educators who came from the southern states to Detroit to attend Wayne State during the summer to take courses that lead to earning the doctor's degree. Many of us local Black students who were interested in doctoral study figured out Wayne State's mentality. Black educators from the South were not considered a threat for positions outside of the South and would use their degrees earned primarily in the South; plus, the South was a good recruitment source.

DOCTORAL STUDY AT THE UNIVERSITY OF MICHIGAN

I then thought that I would inquire about a doctoral opportunity at the University of Michigan. I found out that they had a Doctor of Philosophy Program in Guidance and Counseling that not only served educators, but also persons involved in employment counseling, vocational and occupational guidance and counseling, as well as human resource activities. I inquired about applying for the Ph.D Program. I was told by Dr. Hulslander, the Director of the Counseling and Guidance Education Department, to "come on up and let us see what you can do." I took a couple of summer courses with which I had no problem and formerly applied for the doctoral program. Dr. Hulslander asked me to take several tests. One of note was the Miller Analogy Test, a test that I had never seen or heard of before. I apparently must have done alright because I was asked to provide my transcripts from Wayne State University. I thought that I was ready to begin doctoral study, but I was then told that my work at Wayne State did not meet the requirements at the University of Michigan. I questioned that, having earned a Bachelor of Science and a Master of Education, plus having completed other postgraduate study at Wayne. Dr. Hulslander stated that I did not have an academic major. He said that an academic major was required before I could continue on with the doctoral program at the University of Michigan.

I did go back to Wayne State and took a year, including summers, to complete a graduate academic major in sociology that I presented to Dr. Hulslander to satisfy that requirement and was scheduled into doctoral classes. I was then informed about another necessary requirement that had to be met to earn the Ph.D. The requirement was that I had to have a reading knowledge of two languages related to my course of study that was usually French and German. I then took a school year (two semesters) of French from an excellent instructor who was French to gain a reading knowledge. The test of proficiency was to be given five books of French Pedagogy from any of which I could choose five pages to translate into English. I passed the French test. I did not however, want to have to take German if I could avoid it. I petitioned the graduate Dean to see if I could take something else in place of the second language requirement. The Dean granted my request and allowed that I could take a special course in Survey Research that was only offered during the summer session. The course attracted students from many countries all over the world. It took me two summers to successfully complete the course instead of learning German. While some of this had been taking place, I was still working as a counselor at Burroughs Intermediate School.

I applied to the Detroit Board of Education for a Sabbatical Leave, which was approved. A Sabbatical Leave meant that I would only receive half pay for the time that I was away. The University of Michigan required that doctoral students spend a year on campus, which I had to do. The Sabbatical Leave, of course meant there would be some financial stress for my wife and me with four children and the usual family and household bills that had to be paid. We fortunately had made some plans for the leave by putting away as much money as we could from the previous year's paydays.

I was also blessed to be married to a very wonderful and supportive wife who was a very good money manager and knew how to make good things happen. She not only knew how to manage money, but also how to keep the family well fed. Every ethnicity has foods indigenous to their culture. That was the case with us as African Americans. Delores and I patronized the well-known outdoor Eastern Market in Detroit where farmers rented stalls and brought their produce to the market to sell on weekends. The farmers sold everything from edible produce to puppies and kittens. The farmer's stalls opened at 6 a.m. There we could buy sacks of corn, bushel baskets of collard greens, mustard, turnip greens, spinach, heads of cabbage, beets, potatoes, fresh pork and other meats, and bushels and sacks of other produce at unbelievably low prices for the amount that you could buy.

Commercial fruit produce companies also had stalls that they could not open until about noon where you could purchase dozens of different fruits at a very reasonable price. Delores and I would stock up on what we needed. Delores was a wonderful cook and knew how to preserve food and vegetables to be prepared for food later. The family did not suffer because of not having enough good food to eat. Delores and I also patronized a similar market that was very easy to get to by a trip through the tunnel to Windsor Ontario, Canada where they sold some of their meats and cheeses differently. These, as I reflect, were interesting and adventurous times. We survived the Sabbatical Leave. We were blessed that God Almighty was in the plan. Delores and I always patronized the Eastern Market and the Canadian market until we left Detroit.

I was placed at Joy Junior High School when I returned from Sabbatical Leave. I refused to go back to Burroughs Intermediate School even though the principal wanted me to return because of the initial demeaning attitude he had established toward me. My studies were going very well at the university. I had three more hurdles to get over for the doctorate degree in addition to the classes being taken. I had to pass the counseling laboratory class, pass the preliminary examinations, do a doctoral research project and write a dissertation.

COUNSELING LABORATORY CLASS

The Counseling Laboratory Class LAB taught by Dr. Roeber was usually one of the stumbling blocks for students seeking the doctorate degree for the Counseling and Guidance program. The University of Michigan had high school students and older clients who came to the laboratory from all over Michigan and Ohio for counseling. They became our clients for counselor training. They, of course, were almost all Caucasian.

The counseling laboratory was very professional. The room had a one-way viewing window. Student counselors were observed by other students and Dr. Roeber. Clients did not know that their sessions were being observed or heard. Dr. Roeber graded us on how we established rapport with our clients, how at ease and comfortable we made them feel in accepting us as their counselor and confiding in us, how the counselor picked up leads that the counselee gave us and how much talking the counselor did. Planned silence is a counseling tool. The intent was to get the client to talk. He graded us on how well we knew and used the counseling material in the laboratory, and after the material had been used, how we conveyed the results to the client. The final measurement was the client's acceptance of the counselor and willingness to use the counseling material, if recommended, and return to the laboratory for the results.

Dr. Roeber had a procedure that he used if he thought the counseling session was not going well. The procedure was to knock on the door of the laboratory and tell the student counselor that he had a phone call. Dr. Roeber, or an advanced student would then take over the counseling session. All students who came to the University for counseling received fine counselor attention.

I am pleased to report that I had this class for a year and did very well; so well that Dr. Roeber made me his Graduate Assistant Instructor for which I was paid, and assigned students to prepare them for counseling sessions and recommend a grade.

There were many other classes that were taken in guidance and the understanding of vocational language, professionals in the field and how to analyze the status of opportunities and the preparation necessary to take advantage of them that were being taken. There were also courses in Research Design and Statistics.

PRELIMINARY EXAMINATION

The second hurdle that I had to get over was passing my Doctoral Preliminary Examination (Prelims). This is another point where many doctoral students fail. I had completed all of the classes I was advised to take and the Counseling Laboratory. Students usually determine when they think they are ready to take the Prelims. The Prelims are a composite of everything a student should have learned in reaching that point in the doctoral program. The examination consisted of specific course questions, multiple choice questions, a review of key persons in the field, professional organizations, journals, current research, the latest literature, statistics, research design and whatever other information was felt to be relevant that the student should have learned in the field of Guidance and Counseling.

In Doctoral Study you get to know your major professors quite well because you are with them during much of your time of study. They are like your surrogates. That is why Doctoral Study is so expensive. I asked Dr. Roeber how he would advise me to study for the Prelims. He said go somewhere, take all of your books and notes, hide out and go through them. My darling wife understood. I got a room at the University of Michigan Union where I did some cramming as Dr. Roeber had suggested.

When taking the Prelims, a person is no longer a name. The person becomes a number and is in a room with other students taking Prelims for other disciplines. I remember that my number was 15. I was told that Prelims are not just scored by professors whom you have had, but by all of the professors in the Counseling and Guidance Department; some whom I did not know or had ever had as professors. The test, or course, was a long well-constructed and untimed test that was arranged in sections and took most of the day to complete. The good Lord was once again in the act and I passed the Prelims. There were students in the testing room with me who had taken their Prelims as many as three times and failed. When a student passes Prelims he or she is presented with a certificate like a small degree statement acknowledging victory and eligibility to continue onto the doctorate degree.

DISSERTATION RESEARCH

The third hurdle that I had to get over was the completion of a research project commonly called a dissertation. I was asked to meet with my committee to let them know what kind of project I had in mind. Since I was working at a junior high school in a very integrated disadvantaged area of Detroit, I told the committee that I wanted to do a research project on a "Comparison of Attitudes Toward School, Self Perception, and Achievement of Students in Junior High Schools in Communities of Different Levels of Economic Affluence." The committee laughed at me and said that all of the students in two junior high schools were too large of a universe for my proposed research. The committee suggested that I narrow the research to just the same grade in two junior high schools. That was good, experienced advice. I received permission of Joy Junior High School where I had an office for a Federal Program, "The In School Youth Work Training Project" that I was administering as one of the promotions I had received.

I submitted a request to the Detroit School System for the use of a junior high school in a neighborhood of a high socioeconomic status. I was given Emerson Junior High School on the far West Side of Detroit with a total Caucasian student body and teaching staff. Mr. Walter O. Breed, the school principal, granted permission for his school to be used for the research. Socioeconomic status was based on median income level, median school years completed and percent of persons employed as managerial or professional workers. The Total Action Against Poverty Program based data on the available Census Tract information at the time and personal interviews and research. My doctoral committee approved of the research design. There are many doctoral students who are successful in passing their

Prelims, but go no further due to incomplete research dissertation requirements. They become known as ABDs, "All But The Dissertation." Completing a dissertation takes a ton of work and a considerable amount of financial responsibility.

There was a time when I was approaching the dissertation stage that Delores was pregnant with Darwyn, our youngest child. Delores had at least three false delivery signals that required that I take her to the hospital in the middle of the night and wait for the prognosis. When my wonderful wife did finally deliver, I made a one-day trip to Cleveland, Ohio and back to take our other children to stay with Shirley, the younger of my two sisters, until Delores came home from the hospital. I had a class to attend when Delores was giving birth. My father was at the hospital for me.

The week after Delores came home from the hospital, I was very hyper and restless - so much so that I called my doctor and told him about it. He committed me to St. Joseph Hospital for 12 days for physical exhaustion. Delores had only been home from the hospital for about a week or so during a time when I had to register for fall classes during my hospital stay. I asked her to go to Ann Arbor and register for me. What a loving, wonderful, sweet wife she was to take on that responsibility for me that she knew nothing about so soon after having given birth. My love for her is infinite.

Mildred Lockhart, a wonderful young teenage member of our church, took care of baby Darwyn for us while all of this was happening. At the writing of this book, she is now Dr. Mildred, Ph.D.

The doctors ran many tests, but found nothing wrong with me other than exhaustion. They cautioned that if I ever had the same symptoms again to let them know right away. When I left the hospital, it was like entering a new world. I went back to work, and after a while, did feel some of the same symptoms, but not quite as severe about which I immediately notified my doctor and was hospitalized again for nine days. I have had no other similar effects after that.

The following process and the procedures that had to take place after my Dissertation Research Project was approved by my doctoral committee:

1. Find the questionnaire(s), scales that had the reliability and validity to get the information that I was seeking. I was able to do that with the help of my committee. They recommended the Stern's Need Press Indexes used by the corporate community to research the same information that I was seeking. I had to get approval from its publisher to use the scale. It was, however, very long and extensive. I had the job of shortening it and putting some of its wording at an 8th grade level.

2. I was pleased that the 8th grade homeroom teachers at Joy Junior High School agreed to administer the questionnaires to their students. Likewise, I had to find someone who would administer the questionnaires at Emerson Junior High. Ms. Rowena Wright, a high school and college classmate and family friend, agreed to administer the questionnaires for me at Emerson Junior High School, which was a blessing.

3. The questionnaires had to be scored after being completed at both schools. Fortunately, I found six very intelligent young ladies from the federally funded In School Youth Work Training Project, whom I could legitimately hire during the summer break to record the responses to all of the questions on the questionnaires from all of the students of both schools onto large coding sheets. It was quite a large task. Coming from disadvantaged circumstances, my research assistants did a wonderful job. This further proves that one's situation in life does not have to determine your education, how smart you are or your intellectual capabilities.

4. The completed coding sheets were then given to a person recommended by the University of Michigan with whom we contracted to put the data onto Hollerith cards that were used for a machine to statistically analyze the data.

In the meantime, I was doing the accompanying research for writing the dissertation to present the analysis of the data relative to the hypothesis and sub-hypothesis.

5. After receiving the statistical analysis of the data, I had to complete the writing of my dissertation, including all of the preliminary research, the information received from the analysis and the research conclusions. I was very fortunate to have on my committee Professor M. Clemens Johnson, who taught and loved research and had my research data thoroughly analyzed. I was pleased that my committee accepted the analysis and the completed work.

6. I was then recommended to a person with whom I contracted who specialized in doing the final typing of dissertation papers. The dissertation was typed in classic academic form including: table of contents, list of tables, page references, footnotes and a bibliography.

I had to have 10 hard cover bound copies of the final typed pages that also included the names of my committee and other routine acknowledgements. The copies were for each committee member: one for each of the two schools, one for the Detroit Public School System, and two for myself. This was of considerable expense.

7. The final step was the defense of my research and the conclusions. The date of my defense was listed in university and community media. It was scheduled at the University High School in Ann Arbor, Michigan. Anyone in the academic community or community at large could appear at the school where I was defending my research and

dissertation to challenge or ask questions about it. I was also defending the conclusions to my committee.

If asked, the defense included: the research design, the tool used to get the information, preliminary research data for the dissertation, the hypothesis, sub-hypothesis, and of course, the final conclusions and why they were as analyzed. It was an interesting session. My beautiful and darling wife was downstairs with Darwyn. I was blessed to have been able to get the student assistance I had and someone willing to administer the questionnaires for me. It had taken me almost two years to complete my research and write my dissertation for acceptance by my doctoral committee.

During my defense, the committee decided that we needed to take a break from the session and suggested that I might want to go to the men's room to refresh myself, which I did. When I came back to enter the exam room, the committee members were all standing at the door and holding out their hands to me saying, "Congratulations Dr. Godbold." I couldn't help it. I began to shed a tear. I still tear up when I remember or relay that moment of the story to anyone. No one can ever take that moment from me; the great University of Michigan, I did it!

GRADUATION

I walked across the stage that April of 1967 for graduation held in the University of Michigan Football Stadium. I was the only Black person receiving the Doctor of Philosophy Degree. I was not only proud of myself, but also for my beautiful, lovely wife, who was with me and stood by me all the way throughout this entire ordeal. I will always love her, no matter what. I only wish that my mother could have been there. I also know that I would have made my grandmother proud.

More Life

OAKLAND COUNTY COMMUNITY COLLEGE DISTRICT PROMOTIONAL OPPORTUNITY

I was a friend of Ralph Banfield, a retired Navy captain and fellow doctoral student, who had something to do with the University of Michigan's Naval ROTC Program. He also moonlighted part-time at Washtenaw Community College, a short distance from the university. He must have mentioned my name favorably to Dr. Leland Luchsinger who was the vice president of Washtenaw College, a name of whom I would get to know more of at a future time. Ralph also advised me that the most current activity-taking place in education was the community college movement.

I had planned to return to the Detroit Public Schools and begin a career in Pupil Personnel Services Administration. I happened to read about the Oakland County Community College District (OCCCD) where a new instructional methodology was being used. Naturally, there was interest enough to investigate it, so I checked with the Wayne State University Placement Office and learned that OCCCD was advertising for teaching positions. I had always wanted to be a higher education professor and applied for a position to teach Sociology since my Ph.D. was with a Sociology major as cognate. I supplied the Placement Office with transcripts and all other information pertinent to my application. An interview by Dr. Richard E. Wilson, Provost and Chief Executive Officer (CEO) of the Orchard Ridge Community College/Campus of the multi-college community college/campus district occurred. I must have had a good interview because I was contacted later that day and was asked by Dr. Wilson to consider the position as the Dean of Student Personnel Services at the college instead of a teaching position in Sociology. I was quite surprised and informed him that I would have to discuss the offer with my wife. Before I could give him the results of my

95

discussion with my Delores, Dr. Wilson had called and interviewed her. Delores gave me the go-ahead to accept the position.

ORCHARD RIDGE COMMUNITY COLLEGE

I began at the Orchard Ridge Community College as its first Black administrator and also in the entire OCCCD. I soon learned that Oakland County was one of the three most affluent counties in the United States.

There were several other things that I had to learn, including my supervisory responsibilities. Those responsibilities included supervising an Associate Dean of Counseling and an Assistant Dean of Student Activities. I was also responsible for student registration and the development of a registrationaire that was used at registration to be able to locate students if necessary. I was personally responsible for dealing with student discipline on campus and individually. I also inherited some of the responsibilities of the Dean of Instruction since that position had not been filled at the time I was hired.

Next, I had to learn the college's instructional methodology called the "Audio Tutorial Educational Methodology." It was primarily instruction using a laboratory approach instead of a classroom-based approach. The campus had three or four large classrooms that could hold 75, 150, 250 or 350 students with rear screen viewing technology. Students were assigned to one of these classrooms, but only had to attend for the first three General Assembly Sessions, GASES. It was in the GASES that students met their instructors for the first time and were given an overview of the course that they were taking including requirements, an explanation of the instructional process, how to use the laboratories (LAB) and location of their instructor's office. After that, students were pretty much on their own to use the LABS and their time profitably.

The instructors were to prepare the course material for the students that were recorded on discs, also referred to as tapes. Students were to go to the LAB and check out the discs of the course lectures. The laboratories were huge rooms arranged with shelves that had enclosed desk stations called carrels for privacy. Each carrel had a stationary tape deck that was mounted in it that students used to play the discs and listen to the professor's lectures. As a requirement, the professors had to have several copies of their lectures for their students and classes. Students could listen to and review a lecture as many times as necessary between the hours of between 8 a.m. to 10 p.m. Some students also used the prepared discs to progress as fast as they wanted to and complete a course before the end of a semester, which a number of older students often did. The number of carrels in a LAB was based on an estimation of the number of students who might use the facility each day. The LABS on days around mid-semester and final exam time could become pretty crowded and well used.

Professors' offices were near the laboratory that was being used for the professor's courses. They made it possible for students to meet with them to ask questions, clarify lecture concepts if needed and other course related concerns. Professors provided a sign-up sheet for students who had questions about the course or needed to meet with them to sign for a Small Assembly Session (SAS) of about 15 students.

The instructional methodology also included a Testing Center where professors could deposit course tests for those students who wanted to evaluate a course before the end of a semester. An Associate Dean managed the Testing Center.

The Audio Tutorial Instructional Methodology that was absolutely avant-garde at the time had become widely known. I entertained educators curious about the methodology from many different places including two busloads of educators from Japan.

ORCHARD RIDGE COLLEGE PROVOST AND CHIEF EXECUTIVE OFFICER

I had been at the Orchard Ridge College for approximately 18 or 19 months when I was told by the Provost, Dr. Wilson, that he was resigning. Dr. John Tirrell, President of the OCCCD, had introduced the Audio Tutorial Instructional Methodology. The Board of Trustees had completely accepted and financed the methodology, including the construction of the beautiful Orchard Ridge College Campus. Dr. Tirrell had gotten into a controversy with the Board of Trustees and abruptly resigned. He had a strong and loyal District Administrative Team of which Dr. Wilson was one. Dr. Wilson immediately got another position with the American Association of Junior Colleges (AAJC) in Washington, D.C. The one District Administrator left was Dr. Irving Harlacher. So Dr. Wilson recommended that I be made the Interim College Provost and CEO.

A loyal member of my staff informed me that the college staff was beginning to mount a campaign to determine who should become the College Provost upon hearing of Dr. Wilson's resignation, including a Caucasian Associate Dean on my own staff. In spite of the campaign, I was still appointed the Interim Provost as recommended by Dr. Wilson.

Dr. Wilson was a wonderful mentor and tutor for me, regardless of what other members of the staff thought of him. He introduced me to campus college administration and the national system of community college education. He recommended that I attend student services conventions and those of the American Association of Junior Colleges (AAJC) in which I involved my wife as a partner.

98

As the Provost of the Orchard Ridge Community College, I began to attend the AAJC conventions. I also became a member of a loosely formed group of Black delegates from other colleges to the convention called the Black Caucus. The Black Caucus had an issue with the AAJC about the agency's representation of community colleges that were now a new part of the traditional post-secondary two-year college hierarchy, particularly since the colleges were attracting more Black students. The AAJC stated that a new community college was being established every week; yes, but mostly in the suburbs of cities while two-year colleges in some of our major cities were suffering from neglect. There also arose a Hispanic Caucus.

A representative of the President Nixon Republican Administration who had heard of the Audio Tutorial Instructional Methodology of OCCCD approached me. He invited me to Washington, D.C. twice, once with my wife, in an effort to get me to become President of the new Federal City Community College to implement the Audio Tutorial Methodology at the college that was being established. Federal City Community College was having a very shaky political start. I appreciated the effort, but refused the offer. Federal City Community College did not last very long and later became a four-year college and university.

Dr. Leland Luchsinger, who had become President of the Community College of Denver System, also contacted me. Captain Ralph Banfield must have made me known to him. Dr. Luchsinger told me that he was on his way back to Colorado from the AAJC Convention that was held in Massachusetts and had to change planes at Detroit's Metropolitan Airport. He said that he would like to meet with me at the airport to discuss a matter with him, which I agreed to do. Delores and I met with Dr. Luchsinger and his wife. Dr. Luchsinger said that he would like to have me come to Denver to help him establish the Community College of Denver System. He

99

made me an offer that was considerably less than I was earning at OCCCD. I politely and respectfully had to refuse his offer.

One of the prerequisites of being an administrator in the OCCCD that I learned about after becoming the Provost of the Orchard Ridge College was that spouses of certain administrative positions could take classes without having to pay tuition. Upon notifying my wife of this perk, it created her interest in becoming a student. At the age of 28, Delores enrolled at the college. She had some trepidation about becoming a student because of having only gone to segregated all-Black schools in Washington, D.C. It was at the Orchard Ridge College of the OCCCD that my wife began her higher education. I told those professors who spoke with me to treat her like they did all other students. She soon got over all of her anxieties and became an excellent student. Delores completed her first two years of college at the Orchard Ridge College of the OCCCD. The Audio Tutorial Instructional Methodology was well suited for her with four children, as it was for other students in similar situations. I was, and still am very proud of her.

I did the job of the Provost of Orchard Ridge College with commendations during a period when the Weathermen, The American Youth For Democracy (AYD), and other student activism took place on campus with attempts to interrupt classes and take over the campus. I must acknowledge the assistance and help of a particularly loyal staff member and wonderful person, Dr. Lawrence Gage, who was the Acting Dean of Student Personnel Services during that time.

ACCOMPLISHMENTS

PERSONNEL

I am proud of the fact that during my tenure as the only Black administrator in the district at a college that had one Black faculty member and a librarian when I arrived, that I was able to hire eight Black members to the college staff - an English professor, two sociologists, a science professor, two counselors and an Associate Dean for Testing with a doctoral degree.

PROJECT 50

I also learned that Michigan State University offered a proposal to OCCCD that any of our Black students who successfully graduated from our colleges would be given a scholarship to do the last two years at Michigan State University free of tuition and fees. I was aware of the Rockefeller Talent Search Program for Black students in Detroit. I contacted the director whom I knew. I told him about the Michigan State Proposal. I asked him if he could identify and recommend 50 Black students whom he thought would like the opportunity for a college degree and who he thought could be successful at the community college level. The director made that happen and we enrolled 50 inner city Black youth at the Orchard Ridge College 20 miles from Detroit where maybe, only two or three Black students had previously been enrolled. Most of the White professors never had the experience of teaching or working with Black students. Busing had to be arranged for the students to get to and from the college. There were of course many challenges, both positive and negative. But, other than those faculty and staff whose biases had already been formed, the faculty and staff wonderfully accepted the challenge. They learned a lot about Black people and particularly Black students.

The faculty created an organization entitled "Project 50". They had buttons made that were half White and half Black that were worn to let any of the 50 Black students who needed any kind of help know that they could feel free come to them. There were some student problems, but very few. I am pleased to report that of the 50 Black students recruited over 30 successfully completed their community college education and approximately 25 or more took advantage of the Michigan State University offer and continued their four-year education there. The success of the college faculty and those Project 50 students can be typified by the fact that one of the Black students was elected President of his Orchard Ridge College graduation class.

SELECTION OF NEW OCCCD DISTRICT PRESIDENT

I was asked to have a seat on the selection committee for the new District President. The committee met for many evenings and interviewed a collection of outstanding applicants, one of whom was Dr. Joseph Hill. Dr. Hill, whom I knew as a great intellect and was on the staff at Wayne State University, was selected for the District President's position. During the interview process, he committed to maintaining the innovative reputation and instructional methodology for which the district was known, and was the selling point of his selection. Shortly after his selection, I was given the permanent position of Orchard Ridge College Provost.

Dr. Hill was very personable and became well known and liked by most of the district staff. However, he had another innovative approach that he was espousing to the elimination of the Audio Tutorial Instructional Methodology. He was trying to establish what he called the Educational Sciences (ES). Dr. Hill's theory of the ES was a scientific way that could be used to help students learn. The ES were particularly oriented or specifically related to Black and White or Caucasian students. The theory was that White students were better learners and able to reason abstract material greater than Black students. Black students were objective learners who learned primarily by the senses and native or genetic talent; Black students were born with such objective talent as athleticism and learning acquired by the objective use of the senses of taste, feeling, smelling, hearing and seeing more so than intellectual learning from being able to reason abstractly as could White students. I immediately considered Dr. Hill's theory of the ES to be racist.

Dr. Hill hired a significant number of people for unusual staff positions. He set up a most elaborate, but absurd testing process to test or prove his theory that was ridiculed by much of the staff. How Dr. Hill was going to implement any results derived from the testing process was not known. What impacted me was that Dr. Hill had all but done away with the Audio Tutorial Educational Methodology and was commandeering space on my beautiful campus in an attempt to implement his theory to my dislike.

Dr. Hill was also very treacherous in other ways regarding his staff manipulations. He told us at an administrative staff meeting that he was going to half-fund two positions. One was the Associate Dean For Testing's position on my campus who was hired for the Audio Tutorial Program and the same position on one of the other district campuses. By doing so, he felt that one of the two persons in the position would resign and a position would be made for the person who did not resign. That act was supposed to have been held in confidence by us at that meeting. Since I had hired my Associate Dean for Testing who had a Doctorate Degree, I immediately informed him of what had been proposed to happen. I am pleased to say that my Associate Dean, upon being made aware of what Dr. Hill proposed to do, applied for the position of President of Wayne County Community College that had been announced and was selected.

DECISION TO LEAVE ORCHARD RIDGE AND THE OCCCD

Dr. Luchsinger, President of the Community College of Denver System, still had an interest in hiring me. While back in Michigan attending a conference, he contacted me about still wanting me to join him in Denver. I discussed his offer with my wife as I always did. Understanding what was happening at the OCCCD, she agreed that we should accept Dr. Luchsinger's offer. Delores and I arranged a dinner meeting with Dr. Hill and informed him that I was resigning my position at Orchard Ridge in the OCCCD. Dr. Hill, of course, accepted my resignation. I do not know what happened to Dr. Hill's ES theory or the Audio Tutorial Instructional Methodology after I left the district. I do know that Dr. Hill was the President of the OCCCD for many years and increased the district's number of colleges before his death.

DENVER

The mission of Dr. Luchsinger was to establish three community colleges in three consecutive years. He was still interested in me for three reasons: (1) As mentioned earlier, I had probably been brought to his attention by Captain Ralph Banfield, a fellow doctoral student with me at the University of Michigan when Dr. Luchsinger was the Vice President of Washtenaw Community College. (2) Dr. Luchsinger's interest in the Audio Tutorial Instructional Methodology of the OCCCD. (3) The need to hire a Black campus head or CEO for one of his colleges in Denver.

I began my tenure for the Community College of Denver System on July 1, 1970 to establish the Downtown Auraria Community College Campus. My wife was left to sell our property in Detroit. Until I found a house to buy, I had a room at the Downtown YMCA. I found a good house in a predominantly Jewish neighborhood at 842 S. Holly Street, near George Washington High School and other outstanding schools. The Auraria College Campus was to begin in a vacant automobile dealership building where space had been adapted for classroom and administrative use. This, of course, was a far cry from the beautiful Orchard Ridge College that I had just left, but it was a wonderful administrative experience for me.

I had some things to learn. Dr. Luchsinger was another wonderful mentor. There was one interim staff person at the college who was placed there from the District Office to receive the mail and applications for positions that were to become available until a CEO had been hired.

There was one mistake I made in moving to Denver. That mistake was taking the older of my two daughters out of high school in the 12th grade. It was not a unilateral decision that I made, but I received the emotions of her feelings for that having happened. I hope that she has truly forgiven me for letting that happen.

I was given full reign to develop the educational program from information already determined and select all of the faculty and administrative staff. One of the first administrative positions that I filled was the Director of Admissions and Registration with Mr. Waymond Tinsley, a professional colleague from the Orchard Ridge Community College and with whom I had worked in the Detroit Public Schools System. He was delighted to join me in Denver. The next person whom I hired was a Business Manager, Harold A.W. Tibbs, a retired colonel from the Air Force Academy. He was a well-prepared, wonderful and professional business manager from whom I learned a lot about budgeting and how to use the college's money. Mr. Tibbs' axiom was always to "zero out" the budget and not have to give any of it back. Until I had filled all of the college administrative positions, I served not only as the college CEO, but also as the Dean of other positions with the Business Manager and the Director of Admissions and Registration. With the exception of a few positions, I hired the faculty that I needed to begin the instructional program at the college in September of 1970. We enrolled about 1,000 students.

As the school year progressed, the district office located other buildings near the college that were compatible for student activity use, counseling, administrator and faculty offices. We got along fine and were quite comfortable. I hired Dr. George Yee, who was recommended to me from Detroit, as the Dean of Student Services. I felt that the college needed a Hispanic Dean of Instruction because of a large enrollment of Hispanic students and because I wanted a diverse administrative staff. I went to University Placement Offices in New Mexico, Texas and Colorado to find a Hispanic person with a doctorate degree. I met Dr. Jose Perea at New Mexico University who interviewed well and was interested in the position. I hired him as the Dean of Instruction.

I was able to hire a long-tenured student services professional in Colorado as my Director of Counseling. I also hired star athlete, Ronald Young, who was a graduate of Las Vegas, New Mexico University as my Director of Student Activities. The final required administrative position that I had to fill was Dean of Vocational Education Programs. I was able to hire Donald Goodman, a staff person for the State Board for Community Colleges and Vocational Education, as the College's Dean of Vocational Education Programs. The Deans, of course, supervised and selected their other personnel needs for positions for which I had not selected anyone. The enrollment at the Auraria Community College significantly increased. My entire faculty was hired for the beginning of instruction except for those who had to be hired because of the increase in enrollment. The college soon reached an enrollment of 3,000 students plus. Things were going very well. More faculty members were hired accordingly as need and enrollment increased.

It was because of the increase in students with only three counselors that the Director of Counseling discussed with me the use of the money for one of the counseling positions to hire paraprofessionals to provide routine services, information and staff work related to student needs other than counseling. I thought that was a good idea. This arrangement worked out very well. This was the initiation of the "Team" approach to student services that freed professionally trained counselors to work with students who had serious personal and educational counseling needs.

One of the perks that I was given when hired was five consulting days. I was made aware of a program at the University of Northern Colorado (UNC) called The Center for Special and Advanced Programs, at that time federally funded by the Housing and Urban Development Department. I was hired as an adjunct professor for the program by UNC and able to teach Sociology courses at Gary, Indiana, the Air Force Academy, Camp Pendleton and do some Experiential Counseling in Erie, Pennsylvania. Those were interesting experiences that also helped me to augment my income at a time when my daughter Michelle was a student at Colorado University.

THE INTRODUCTION OF INSTRUCTIONAL LABORATORIES

INDIVIDUALIZED SELF-PACED INSTRUCTION

At Auraria, I had introduced a laboratory instructional education program that related to individualized instruction. I did this along with establishing two instructional laboratories that were presented to the Colorado State Board for Community Colleges and Vocational Education by Dr. Leland Luchsinger.

The Vestibule Laboratory that served as an entry point into the community college for marginal and sub-marginal students, dropouts of all ages, functional illiterates and older students returning to college after years of being away. The activities of the Vestibule Laboratory were analytical, diagnostic, remedial, prescriptive and individualized.

The developmental laboratory was presented as a laboratory that served students who had progressed beyond the vestibule and who were on a curricular course who needed additional instructional assistance. The development laboratory provided a uniquely tailored learning facility for students who desired additional instruction enrichment in various subject matters areas arranged with subject matter instructors.

I also introduced an individual English Tutorial Program for Hispanic students who wanted to become more literate in English.

Another aspect of my Instructional Laboratory Program was that students enrolled in classes and could not keep up with the class instruction could let their instructor know that they needed to use the LABS for help with the course, particularly math and science. The instructor could deposit his or her material in the LAB and the student would be tutored until he or she felt capable of passing the course instructor's test, not the LAB instructor's test, even though the course semester had ended. The student was kept from dropping the class and received course credit. The Laboratory Individualized Instructional approach had to be approved by the State Board in order to qualify for State Apportionment. Lieutenant Governor John D. Vanderhoof was invited to Auraria and I explained the instructional processes of the LABS. He was impressed and recommended the LAB approach for approval to the State Board for the district to receive apportionment.

Metropolitan State College (now University), that had begun as a community college before becoming a four-year institution, accepted my wife's credits from the OCCCD for admission as a junior. After we had gotten settled, she began her courses with a major in Sociology. She was a dedicated and good student and did very well. Delores completed her last two years at Metropolitan State University and graduated with a Bachelor of Arts Degree with a minor in Speech Pathology in 1973.

THE AURARIA HIGHER EDUCATION CENTER PROJECT

Discussions were being held about plans for an Auraria Higher Education Center on which site would be The University of Colorado Denver Center, Metropolitan State College and the Auraria Community College. I had not known about these plans before taking my position in Denver. The colleges on the site agreed that there would be a reciprocity agreement between the colleges; that is, a course taken and passed with a certain grade at one of the colleges would be accepted at the college or university in which a student was enrolled for a degree. The Auraria Higher Education site and agreement of reciprocity sounded like a great idea.

I was invited to attend several of the site planning meetings with Dr. Luchsinger who represented the Auraria Community College on the Site Development Committee, and a few other meetings for him that he could not attend. One of the persons on the Development Committee was a member of the Coors Beer family who was a forceful and powerful committee member. I did not particularly like how my college was being thought of, or how I was treated. I particularly did not appreciate questions about the competency of my staff, where my faculty had gotten their degrees, research they had done, what papers they had written, who was most qualified to manage the Learning Resources Center and how the sharing of facilities on the site would be. I began to feel that Dr. Luchsinger had not been very forceful on the committee, and what I had to say did not mean very much. I also began to feel that my college was going to, so to speak, get the short end of the stick. I wondered about the future of my college and my professional status and tenure if I remained in Denver, a place that I truly began to appreciate so much that I have said it is one of the best places I have ever lived for my family and children.

LIFE IN DENVER, COLORADO

The older of my two daughters, Michelle, graduated from George Washington High School and was accepted at the University of Colorado in Boulder where she attended for two years before coming to Oakland to be with Delores and me. Donald Terrence Juan became a junior high school activist, one of the most outstanding high school athletes in the State of Colorado and Student Leader at George Washington High School where 300 Black students were bussed in. Don was a leader among the Black students and well liked by many of his high school classmates. Don continued his athletic ability in track at the University of California at Davis where he was to have been invited for a tryout for the USA Olympic Team until surgery was necessary on one of his knees. Darwyn, my younger son also showed some athletic ability in his little league. He was called the "Floyd Little" of his league, named after the star Denver Bronco player at that time. Monique, the younger of my two daughters was well liked at her junior high school and became a member of the Camp Fire Girls organization of which I was a member of the Board of Directors for a while. She also busied herself with finding a church for us to attend since there was no church like ours in Denver.

Denver at that time was a wonderful place to raise children. I bought bicycles for Delores and me and we went bike riding practically everyday. We went on two 30-mile bike trips initiated by the Community College of Denver staff. I bought skis for the whole family. We were taught how to ski by one of my faculty members. I was also a member of the Board of Directors of the Denver Urban League.

The staff of our community college district also arranged two white water rafting trips, one down the Yampa River on which Delores and I went, and the other down the Colorado River through the Grand Canyon that Delores did not want to go. My youngest daughter Monique wanted to go, so she joined me instead. The Colorado River white water rafting trip was for several nights, 90 miles through the

Grand Canyon that began at Flagstaff, Arizona where Monique and I drove from Denver to meet our group and board our raft. When the river trip was completed, it took a whole day to climb out of the canyon because of a switch back trail that had to be used to climb up to get out of the canyon. Everyone was exhausted. The climb was so difficult, hot and draining that after reaching the top I let Monique have the pleasure of a cold beer for the first time. A couple of women climbing up to the top at the same time did so topless. Monique thoroughly enjoyed the trip and often speaks of it as one of the most eventful activities of her life. It was a trip that was a wonderful bonding experience for me with my Monique at the age of 14 or so.

Living in Denver was a wonderful professional and family experience. I became the leader of the Black Caucus at the American Association of Junior Colleges (AAJC) and a group of Black delegates, primarily administrators, who brought about a change in the entire AAJC organization. We were able to get Black college presidents elected to the formerly all-White Board of Directors and several other organizational changes. Dr. Rosetta Wheadon and I wrote the first Constitution and bylaws for the Council on Black American Affairs, the name that I gave the Black Caucus. I became the first council member to have a seat on the AAJC Board of Directors, a position that I took seriously. I began the use of official stationery by the council that I had my Graphic Arts instructor design for the council logo and the stationery letterhead. As an AAJC Board member, I was held accountable by the AAJC that the council could financially support its business and organization activities.

AURARIA HIGHER EDUCATION CENTER PROGRESS AND STATUS

My concern about the Auraria Higher Education Center and the future of my college increased as the project began to take shape

111

with all of the faculty and staff's activism. It just so happened that I was contacted by Dr. Norvel Smith, President of Merritt College, whom I had met when attending the AAJC and had become a part of the Black Caucus that I previously stated had some differences with the AAJC. Dr. Smith informed me that he was leaving Merritt College for a position at the University of California at Berkeley. He encouraged me to apply for the Merritt College presidency. He called me several times and sent me an application. He said that he wanted to have a hand in picking his successor. I completed and submitted the application, though I really was not excited about going to California and knew little about Oakland. I had been invited as a consultant to participate in a Black Studies Workshop at Los Angeles City College when I was with the Orchard Ridge College in Michigan. I also participated in a 15-day workshop for new college presidents that Dr. Luchsinger let me attend while in Denver. It was conducted by Dr. Lamar Johnson and his wife at the University of California at Los Angeles. I was really not very impressed with Los Angeles.

A committee interviewed me twice for the position at Merritt College, with faculty representatives, then by the full Board of Trustees. Dr. Thomas Fryer, Chancellor of the Peralta Community College District at the time, called me around 11:00 p.m. Denver time to let me know that the Peralta Board of Trustees had selected me for the Merritt College position and wanted to know if I wanted it. I had a brief consultation with Delores, and we accepted the position. Delores and I arranged a meeting with Dr. Luchsinger at his home, and with some feelings of remorse after all that he had done for me, and informed him that I had accepted the Merritt College position. It was a professional move that I have lived to regret.

There are two axioms that I would like to leave with readers of this book. First, in making a professional move of some significance, vet the place and position as much as you are being vetted for the position. I had neither heard of nor knew anything about the Peralta

112

Community College District before moving to Oakland to take the Merritt College position. Secondly, do not always listen to a friend, no matter how close the friend may be because you are not always given the whole truth, which I was not. I should have asked Dr. Smith for the whole truth of why he was leaving the presidency of Merritt College.

California Love

CALIFORNIA

MERRITT COLLEGE

I began my tenure at Merritt College in October of 1973. I had a lot to learn about the community college system in California that I found differed from other states, but also differed in different areas within the state. I found a college with a good faculty and excellent teaching that considered itself to be an elite educational institution that I was told was the "Little Harvard of the West." However, I soon found out, as was told to me by one of Merritt's faculty members, Ms. Pearlina Hill, that Merritt was nothing but a "glorified high school." I agreed. I was a well-educated and experienced community college administrator at a level of education in which I truly believed to be valuable. I had not come to California to be a high school principal.

What I found:

The college operated on the K-12 administrative system

Students did not pay tuition

Student enrollment was determined by Average Daily Attendance (ADA) as was used for K-12

An ineffective and inefficient budgeting system

The president's office had no budget

A hostile and anti-administration faculty

Dr. Smith, who had done a good job of dealing with members of the Black Panther Party at the college while he was president, had mostly let the Dean of Instruction administer the college.

There was an inefficient and ineffective Instructional Council composed of faculty department chairpersons excused from teaching one class to manage the department's business, and some curriculum coordinators.

The Dean, a line administrator, said that he was only a vote in decisions made by the council.

A college hostile with other district colleges and the district office.

A hybrid of Berkeley and Oakland High School faculty members that did not relate to higher education or believe in professional travel or other higher education demeanor.

I soon learned that my pedigree would be tested on how I dealt with the district office and that Merritt operated on the basis of college autonomy. In order to become a community college, Merritt, once called Oakland City College, had to become affiliated with the Berkeley Trade School and offer occupational programs. I sensed this was not the most appreciated by the so-called academic side of the faculty because of issues brought to me by some of the vocational faculty. I settled in for a while before I made the effort to organize Merritt as a Community College as I knew them to be.

I was helped to get "settled in" at Merritt by local clergy who invited me to breakfast and knew of the community activities of the college that included the beginning and the organizing of the Black Panther Party. Merritt was well known to the clergy who offered their support to me as President. Prominent among the clergy was Reverend J. Alfred Smith who sought to help us locate the kind of Church in

Oakland to which we belonged. That, of course, did not happen. We, as a family, were invited to attend the services of Allen Temple Baptist Church pastored by Reverend Smith at which we were given a warm welcome and also enjoyed the services. My son, Donald, was also hired by the church to be the principal of its summer school program. We have continued to attend and support Allen Temple for approximately 40 years without relinquishing our membership in the Churches of God Holiness in which Reformation my wife was raised.

COLLEGE BUDGET

First, I began to straighten out the budgeting process and let the Business Manager know that he worked for me as the President and not that I was subject to him for what I needed or wanted. I also informed him that I would be involved in the development of the college budget. I soon learned that whenever I wanted budget information, he could not give me specifically what I wanted, but his staff assistant, who was apparently more knowledgeable about the college budget than he was, could.

Chairpersons on the Instructional Council were given an amount of budget money that they would wait until near the end of the fiscal year to use that would then be charged to the succeeding or next year's budget reducing the availability of funds from the new budget. The management of the college budget also resulted in unspent budget money being returned to the District Administration. I informed the Business Manager that I believed in "zeroing out" the budget and not giving anything back to the District. I taught him and his assistant how to do that by limiting all spending at about April and reconciling all unspent money into one pot for reallocation. The process worked very well. It worked so successfully that we were able to use the unspent money to purchase "small stores," notebooks and other paper supplies, etc., air conditioners for the portables and other capital needs from the current year's budget.

COLLEGE REORGANIZATION

I arranged a meeting with the entire faculty to inform them that I planned to organize the college by Academic Divisions which, of course, they had some questions. I did get some support from a faculty member, Dr. Suzanne Adams, which I appreciated. I did not "railroad," or "dictate" the reorganization, but worked cooperatively with the Faculty Senate leadership to arrive at a consensus agreement that the person who became a Division Administrator would have to teach a class. The Instructional Council was eliminated. The Dean of Instruction was to perform his line responsibilities and supervise the Divisional Reorganization and the Administrators. It was after one year of the reorganization that I was approached by the Division Administrators who were given the title of Assistant Deans about the administrative workload that was interfered with by having to teach a class. I again worked with the Academic Senate Leadership to get an agreement with them that the one class that had to be taught by Division administrators be dropped. The Academic Senate Leadership signed both of the agreements for the Divisional Reorganization.

PROFESSIONAL HIRING PROCESS

I informed the Dean of Instruction that I was going to establish a hiring process that took nothing away from the faculty or him as Dean, but that involved both Deans and the President. The process would be that position applicants be interviewed by a diverse faculty committee. Qualified applicants who successfully got through the faculty interview, be further interviewed by the appropriate Dean and the President, or of whom any two, three, up to five who were interviewed and determined to be acceptable for a position if any one were to be hired, be recommended to the appropriate Dean, and me if the position was in the Dean's area of supervision. I thought that was reasonable and a Dean could advocate for the person he or she felt most qualified and best for the position. I felt that this being a community college the President ought to know something about a person who was being hired as a member of the faculty. The Dean of Instruction resigned from his position.

COLLEGE DEANS APPOINTMENTS

I made a mistake of which I will take responsibility. I hired a new Dean of Instruction who was a person of color and already the Dean of a college in the Peralta District. I also promoted the existing Assistant Dean, who would have been considered the heir apparent to the position of Dean of Instruction, to the new position of Dean of Administration and Development. He appeared to get along well with the faculty and worked well with me. I wanted him to extend his efforts to initiate and implement a beginning program of Laboratory Instruction of which he would be in charge. I did not make these appointments unilaterally. I did so with the approval of Dr. Fryer the District Chancellor. My mistake was in not announcing the positions. By not announcing the positions, I incurred the ire of the college faculty for which acts they sued me. A suit that did not stand up in court.

The new Dean of Administration and Development was able to develop an instructional learning laboratory as the initial effort of developing a complete Instructional Laboratory Educational Methodology that was given the name of the Learning Assistance Laboratory.

MERRITT COLLEGE GRADUATION POLICY

When I arrived, Merritt had a graduation policy that the students had activated for and got approved. In order to graduate, students had to take one of the courses related to students of color: Black, Hispanic, Asian or Native American. A Caucasian faculty member met with me and told me that she had been raised as a Methodist, but had learned that her heritage was Jewish and she wanted Jewish studies to be included with those that students had to take for graduation. I did not give her an immediate answer because the graduation requirement was in effect when I arrived and it was something for which students had activated as a college policy. I referred the request to my new Dean of Instruction who established a committee composed of faculty, concerned members of the community Non-Jewish, White, Black, Jewish, Jewish organizations and students. The committee scheduled meetings for approximately a year and a half that came to the conclusion that Jewish Studies should not be included with those related to students of color for graduation. I accepted that conclusion. The report was given to Dr. Fryer, District Chancellor. Dr. Fryer called me and asked if I accepted the report. I told him that I had, and the graduation requirement, as it was when I arrived at Merritt, would continue to be the policy. A Jewish study class was already being offered at the college for students to take if they wanted to, but not as a requirement for graduation. A Jewish Studies course was, however, made a requirement for graduation at another college of the district.

STUDENT ACTIVISM

CHILD CARE CENTER

About 40 students invaded my office with signs that read something like, "thou shall be on the side of the child" about the need for a Child Care Center closer to the college instead of one that was some distance away at a church. I was able to bring this to the attention of the District Office and work with them to negotiate the building of a very up-to-date model Child Care Center using college space.

BLACK STUDENT MOVEMENT

I was asked by Bobby Seale to be the speaker at the 8th grade graduation of the Black Panther School, which I accepted. Remnants of the Black Panther Party were still students on campus who approached me about having the District Administration return $40,000 they said had been taken from them. Due to its initial K-12 administration and no tuition, Merritt did not have a student activity fee program. This was atypical of most community colleges, but Merritt students had organized into clubs and other student organizations on their own. The Black Student organization that included Black Panthers was astute enough to become incorporated and was the only incorporated community college student body organization in California. The $40,000 that the students claimed had been taken from them, I was told was used by the district Administration to make a down payment on the Student Center. All of the student facilities, food service, bookstore and student center literally and officially belonged to the Merritt incorporated student body organization. This was a problem that I had to contend with and try to handle.

MAOIST STUDENT TAKE OVER

There were also the Maoist members of the student body who tried to take over the student newspaper and who also invaded my home. I was given a surprise birthday party by members of my staff. A student of the Maoist group saw the note about it on a secretary's desk and told other students who invited themselves and students from the other District colleges to the party who came in vans. Of course the party was disrupted and did not continue.

These are but a few of the problems that I had to deal with while President of Merritt College. There were more.

THE NATIONAL COUNCIL ON BLACK AMERICAN AFFAIRS

When I arrived at Merritt College, I was still on the Board of Directors of the AAJC. It was surprising that no one at the college or in the Peralta Community College District had heard of the Council on Black American Affairs (COBAA) after those of us who were members of the AAJC Black Caucus had worked so hard to get Dr. Norvel Smith on the Board of Directors.

I continued my leadership of the COBAA. Here is what I did:

> Traveled across the country to meet with Black employees of community colleges to organize the COBAA nationally according to accreditation areas.

> My college in Denver, Colorado did not want to be a part of the North Central Association Accreditation area, but wanted to be a part of the Western Association of Schools and Colleges area.

> Established the Western Region of the COBAA and appointed George Herring as the President. While President, George traveled with me to other college districts on the mission of the COBAA. John Greene, President of Merritt College succeeded George Herring as President.

> Initiated and started successful regional conferences that were held in Berkeley, Los Angeles, Monterey and Seattle.

> The Western Region conferences were the model for conferences in the other regions. I was the speaker at the conferences in every organized region on behalf of the COBAA.

> I also sent invoices to community colleges throughout the country for a $100 membership in the National COBAA.

To make a long story short, I established and organized the National Council on Black American Affairs from my community college in Denver and Merritt College. There are some witnesses to what is being reported who are still alive.

VICE CHANCELLOR OF EDUCATIONAL SERVICES

The Peralta Board of Trustees must have been pleased with my work at Merritt. While on a business trip with which I also planned a small vacation, I received a call from the President of the Peralta Board of Trustees who asked me if I would consider being appointed to the position of District Vice Chancellor of Education Services. I asked the President to allow me to discuss the offer with my wife, as I always did, along with my family. The decision of the family was not unanimous, but I listened to my wife and accepted the offer. I felt that I was leaving Merritt with some unfinished business, but had helped Merritt become a Community College in the truest sense. I left my mark.

The District Faculty was upset and directed their hostility toward me because, again, the position was not advertised. That was a status directed at me for the rest of my tenure in Peralta. I left Merritt College with no great fanfare.

I became the District Vice-Chancellor of Educational Services in November of 1977. The position required a learning and adaptive process. I received the ire of the college president of one of the district's local colleges and some of the upper administrative staff who let me know in words of no uncertain terms that they would not respect my authority in the position. I received that same admonition from the vitriolic and extremely blatant racist president of Feather River College, Peralta's distant community college in Quincy, California at that time. In spite of this unpleasant and somewhat hostile environment, I performed my duties very professionally and

123

did a very respectable job with most of the staff at the District Office.

Soon upon moving into the Vice Chancellor's position, I was able to defuse a dispute about the use of district money by the Director of Community Services of one of the district's colleges for contracting with a Boy's Catholic Choir to perform at the college. In the district this was considered the inappropriate use of district money in support of a religious activity.

Chancellor Fryer left the Peralta Community College District to take a similar position at a neighboring community college.

OFFICE OF INSTITUTIONAL ANALYSIS AND DEVELOPMENT

As the Vice Chancellor of Educational Services, I established the office of Institutional Analysis and Development to determine how district instructional money was being spent and also to assist District Faculty and staff with the development of proposals for program funding. We found that there were faculty without a full load, colleges with unfilled positions and the ethnic composition of our student body that could relate to proposal development for additional financial resources. The functions and purpose of the office, of course, were questioned because it was getting pretty close to what was taking place at the colleges.

PERALTA'S ATTITUDE CONCERNING EMPLOYEES

I started a program called Peralta's Attitude Concerning Employees (PACE). The one thing about the Peralta District at the time was that you had to accept the staff that you inherited. The District Office had some staff that were noticeably not good for work for several hours in the afternoon because of the consumption of alcohol at lunch. One of whom was the person who became my secretary. The president of the Board of Trustees who was a Probation Officer was

124

made aware of my concern, but would not let me find another position for her because she came to work early every day and functioned well in the morning. He said that she was a "functional alcoholic" and to make any changes with her would only make her condition worse. I was at a professional luncheon meeting hosted by Kaiser Industries and was talking with one of the table guests whose job was working with Kaiser employees who had similar personal problems. She gave me the name of a county organization that Peralta could contract with for a fee. Employees could confidently be given help with a number of personal problems, like alcoholism, without the employer knowing when and how often they were being seen. I contracted with the organization and made their information known to all of the employees of the Peralta Community College District.

BANKING AND SMALL BUSINESS

I was able to get two pilot instructional programs started in the district that were requested by the community: the Banking Program that was offered at Laney College and the Small Business Administration Program that was offered at Vista College. I continued to professionally manage my other position-related responsibilities in a somewhat unfriendly environment.

A NEW CHANCELLOR IS HERE

The position of Chancellor of the Peralta Community College District was announced. I was encouraged to become an applicant for the position. The district had a policy that anyone in the district could apply for any position announced. The selection process also included the establishment of a large comprehensive committee composed of faculty, administrators and students that applicants had to get past to have an interview with the Board of Trustees. The students selected were usually and very deliberately adult members of the committee who had been well prompted about how to vote. Four

Black administrators were on the committee when I was interviewed. Three of the Black administrators voted for me, but one did not. He had been the president of the Black Arkansas A&M College until it was integrated and he lost his job with the parent Arkansas University, and was hired as a president of one of the district's colleges by the Peralta Chancellor. He wanted to gain brownie points with the White members on the committee the old fashioned southern way. This was not very intelligent politics on his part because I was not going to be passed on to the Board of Trustees for an interview anyway. I was not passed on for an interview, which in discussion with some of the Trustees was absurd since they had appointed me to the position of Vice Chancellor for Educational Services without announcing it. They felt that I should not even have had to go before that committee to have gotten an interview with the Trustees.

Interviews for the District Chancellor position were held. Mr. Max Tadlock, a former College Dean who had become a well-known consultant, was selected. Max Tadlock was very personable and became well liked. In accepting the position he agreed to close out his consulting activities that required considerable time away from the district. Knowing that I had been an applicant for the Chancellor position, he met with me after his selection and asked me what I planned to do now since I was an applicant and had not been selected. I simply told him that I planned to continue my job at Peralta and had no plans to leave. I assured him that in doing my job I had no resentment about him being selected and would support his administration.

Chancellor Tadlock and I had a good relationship. He agreed with the establishment of the Office of Institutional Analysis and Development and even used one of the staff members of the office in his consulting business that he continued to do. He involved me in the process of selecting District Office personnel, particularly the

Director of Human Resources. When Chancellor Tadlock would leave his office on a consulting trip with his oversized briefcase of materials, he would come by my office, peek in and simply say, "You've got the duty," which meant that I was in charge of the District while he was gone. There was an occasion or two when he would arrive back in the district hours before a board meeting and was unprepared, so I would have to help him when certain agenda items were discussed.

I believe that the political climate of the Peralta Community College District was a bit much for Chancellor Tadlock. I also believe that he was regularly confronted by the District Academic Senate about me, but had no recourse because I did my job, supported him, saved him on occasion and had the support of the Board of Trustees.

Chancellor Tadlock held the Chancellor position for about two-and-a-half years before he left the Peralta Community College District to become the President of Monterey Peninsula Community College where he had once been a Dean. Chancellor Tadlock and I remained friends after he left the district.

SELECTION OF THE PERALTA COMMUNITY COLLEGE DISTRICT CHANCELLOR THE SECOND TIME

The position of District Chancellor was again announced. Once more I was encouraged to apply. This time the Peralta Board of Trustees hired a Community College Consultant, Dr. Karl Drexler. Peralta had a normal-sized representative selection committee of faculty, administrators and possibly a student to assist the consultant with the selection. I was imminently prepared and was recommended to the Board of Trustees for an interview. Of course I was not the only candidate recommended to the board; but the use of a professional consultant made the process much more professional, objective and fairer than formerly. I was selected as the Chancellor of the Peralta Community College District.

I began my tenure as the Peralta Community College District Chancellor in August of 1980. Again, I inherited my office staff, but began to improve administrative processes that needed work due to the concept of "college autonomy" that had not served students well. I implemented timely receipt of college transcripts, a much needed Risk Management program for a district of five colleges and outreach centers for student and staff safety in a district where two campus murders occurred, essential staff hiring, two college presidents and two Vice Chancellors to fill District Office vacancies during my tenure.

I would like to add this caution to those of you reading this book who aspire to become an administrator: Try not to ever appoint anyone to an important position who reports to you and is supportive of you, but has to learn how to manage the position on the job.

STUDENT ACCOUNTABILITY MODEL (SAM)

As a former Special Education teacher, I was always interested in student learning and progress. I introduced the Student Accountability Model (SAM) concept, a voluntary student program to assist the 25% of community college students who indicate that they want to go on to a four-year college after completing community college, but never do because they do not become academically prepared. I believed that I accomplished much of what I started out to do during my tenure as Chancellor with the usual routine of business in an antagonistic and hostile environment.

PERALTA TRUSTEE BOARD MEMBER ATTRITION

The Peralta Community College District had a policy that members of the Board of Trustees who had been on the board for 12 years would receive their health care benefits paid for by the district for life. Two long time members of the board took advantage of that policy and decided not to run for reelection. Another member who became a cancer victim and was hospitalized for a while died. A fourth member of the board who was a Military Veteran, put himself into a hospital for psychological reasons resigned from the board. The faculty recruited members for the Board of Trustees whom they supported and got them elected.

STUDENT TUITION AND DISTRICT DEFICIT

Two events occurred that greatly affected the welfare of the Peralta District - the process of charging student tuition, and the failure of a federally funded Vocational Training Skill Center for which Peralta was the Delegate Agency. It was a success under the Democratic Administration, but suffered when the Republican Administration came into office with the process of "Revenue Sharing."

The student tuition fee was approved too late after the April and May dates for the district to take the personnel action necessary to legally reduce faculty and other professional staff. It also caused a significant decline in full-time equated (FTE) students. This meant that we had excess faculty who were under loaded because of the student attrition, a loss of students, whom we had to pay that created a budget problem.

THE EAST BAY EDITH AUSTIN SKILL CENTER

A former Chancellor had been cautioned about putting any district money into the Skill Center by his Vice Chancellor of Administration. He did not take that advice, but did put a few thousand dollars into the Skill Center operation. The Skill Center had lost training programs because of Revenue Sharing and the inability to meet contractual obligations. It became a financial albatross for the Peralta District. Due to minimal financial support, the Skill Center faculty and staff wanted to become a formal part of the Peralta Community College District, which was not financially feasible. I had lost my majority on the Board of Trustees and the new majority would not take my advice when I advised them to close the Skill Center to relieve the district of the debt that it was incurring. The district would not have incurred any obligation to the Skill Center faculty and staff, financially or otherwise, by closing it. They would not close the Center, which increased the financial deficit the district was already facing that caused them to have to borrow money from the state. I believe that the new board majority deliberately did not close the Skill Center and put the district in financial jeopardy as an act against me. The Board of Trustees closed the Skill Center one week after I resigned.

The new majority on the board was able to co-opt an important member of my three-person office staff to get her to accept the responsibility of Secretary to the Board as an act to limit my authority. It was a responsibility of the Chancellor. I was broadsided at the close of a Board meeting when it was announced that she had accepted the offer. Her acceptance was an egregious act of disloyalty. A faculty member approached me after the meeting and said of my staff member's acceptance that, "...there are few times in a person's life when they have the chance to show a little class; she missed it."

I was the Peralta Community College District Chancellor for approximately seven and a half years. I believe that I performed my job duties well considering the environment in which I had to work. I greatly appreciate the District Board of Trustees that selected me for every position that I had in the Peralta Community College District: Merritt College President, Vice Chancellor of Educational Services and Chancellor. They knew the circumstances with which I was dealing with and supported me throughout my tenure in the district.

I could not believe that the other two members of my office staff, for whom I had done much, were unaware of what was taking place. But they did not let me know.

I never said another word to my disloyal staff member.

DARK DECISIONS

I decided to resign my position as Chancellor of the Peralta Community College District because I had lost the balance of the Board of Trustees that had appointed me to the position. I had also come to the conclusion that I had taken enough abuse of being sued (which I always won), demeaned publicly at board meetings, and in the newspapers and the show of egregious disloyalty of at least one of my office staff that thwarted me from being able to do my job. It was beginning to bear on me emotionally and psychologically. I resigned the position of Chancellor and left the office effective July 15 1987. I officially relinquished the title of Chancellor in February of 1988.

THE MORNING SUN

After the rain, the weather always gets better. And after leaving the Peralta Community College District, I was honored to have been offered the position of the Executive Director of the Scotlan Youth and Family Counseling Center, Inc. in the neighborhood of West Oakland. The Center was a "community based non-profit agency" that was primarily funded by the Alameda County Probation Department. The agency provided emergency counseling for problem youth considered "status offenders" up to 18 years of age who were brought to the Center by the police. The counseling provided for the youth and the family was to prevent young folk from becoming "juvenile delinquents," and to reunite the youth with their family. The family, in many instances, also needed some serious counseling. When a youth reached 18 years of age his record at the center was destroyed.

The Scotlan Center also had a very successful education program for which the Center was given a grant by the Oakland Private Industry Council where I also served as a member of the Board of Directors.

During my tenure as the Executive Director of the Scotlan Center, I was able to begin a Parenting Program for women who had been brought to the attention of the center because of substance abuse problems and had their children taken from them by social work authorities. The program was funded by money from the Aid For Dependent Children Program (AFDC) of the State Of California to which agency I wrote the proposal for the grant. The Program gained wide acclaim. Parents were directed to the Parenting Program for certification that they had received rehabilitation treatment for their substance abuse problems. This was an intermediary procedure to prove to social work authorities of a parent's stability and worthiness for their children to be returned to them.

I worked at the Scotlan Center for at least 10 years where I was appreciated and well-respected by the staff, the Board of Directors, the Probation Department and the community before I retired.

Acknowledgements

Legacy

LEGACY

I penned this book as a written testimony and autobiographical legacy of my life of educational achievement, accomplishments and concern for others.

I leave this testimony for my Nuclear Family, those who might read it and posterity. It is a testimony of how I have been blessed, as a motherless child, who, but by the Grace of God, had to make many decisions for himself with the wise advice and counsel of a strong grandmother and support of a loving and caring family.

The legacy that I leave, as I was raised, is to always be a good and responsible person of quiet demeanor and resolve of few words, without the arrogance of intelligence and self-aggrandizement, and with respect for others. That is the life that I have attempted to live.

FAMILY AND EDUCATIONAL ACCOMPLISHMENTS

I leave this legacy for my wife, Delores Roxanna, a wonderful and supportive wife whom I have loved, at the time of this writing for 64 years, who has a B.A. degree in Sociology from Metropolitan State University in Denver, Colorado, and a M.A. degree in Speech Pathology and Audiology from San Francisco State University.

Michelle Roxanne, the older of my two daughters, an accomplished and skilled teacher, who has a B.A. degree in English from the University of California at Berkeley, and a M.A. degree in Education with an emphasis in Child Life from Mills University in Oakland, California.

Donald Terrence Juan, the older of my two sons, who has a B.A. Degree in Psychology from the University of California at Davis, a M.A. degree in Clinical Psychology from San Francisco State

University, a Medical Doctor's Degree from Michigan State University and a Physician's Executive Master of Business Administration Degree (PEMBA) from the University of Tennessee. Donald's wife, Effie, is a registered nurse and nurse administrator and a blessed member of the Godbold family; Lisa Thornton, MD, former daughter-in-law.

Monique Toi, the younger of my two daughters, who was a commissioned officer in the U.S. Army, discharged with the rank of captain, and who has a B.S. degree in Chemical Engineering from the University of Texas, and a Medical Doctor's degree from the University of Michigan; Mark Nassy, MD from the University of Michigan, Systems Engineer.

Darwyn Eugene the younger of my two sons is a U.S. Army Veteran, a Journeyman in the Construction Industry and a Licensed Contractor.

GRANDCHILDREN AND GREAT GRANDCHILDREN

My Grandchildren:

Jessica Reilly, Graduate of Sam Houston University in Houston, Texas, B.A. degree in Industrial Design, Magna Cum Laude with Honors.

Donald Andrew, Mother, Lisa Thornton MD, Drafted by the Los Angeles Dodgers Baseball Team in 2014; student at South East Louisiana University.

Christian Thomas, Professional Chef

Sarah Michelle, Senior at Sacramento State University

Adrien

Aaron

Nyla Rachael

Alexander James

Great Grandchildren, Parents, Jessica and John Reilly

Preslyn

Sienna

John

Great Grandchildren, Parents, Corida and Christian Thomas Godbold

Noah Donald

Miles Howard

Great Grandchildren, Xavier Amir, Parents, Maimoona and Aaron Godbold

My Children, Grandchildren, Great Grandchildren, in-laws, posterity, and others who may read this book should have few if any questions about the genealogy and history of the nuclear family of Donald Horace Godbold, Ph.D. shared with Delores Roxanna Godbold.

God has truly blessed me. It should be obvious that I am very proud of my family and how the Lord has blessed us all.

STILL WATERS RUN DEEP

ABOUT THE AUTHOR
Donald H. Godbold Ph.D.

Dr. Godbold received the Bachelor of Science Degree, in Special
Education from Wayne State University in Detroit, Michigan, where
he also earned the Master of Education Degree, in Educational
Counseling, and the Educational Specialist, Certificate for Post-
Graduate Study beyond the M.Ed. Dr. Godbold also established Post-
Graduate academic majors in Sociology and Educational Psychology,
prerequisite for the study of the Doctor of Philosophy Degree, Ph.D.
at the University of Michigan, U of M. Dr. Godbold earned the Ph.D.
at the U of M in Educational Counseling and Guidance with the
Sociology Cognate. Dr. Godbold was a Clifford Woody Memorial
Scholar, for outstanding promise in professional education, and was
selected for the Leonard F. Saine Esteemed Black Alumnus Award at
the University of Michigan. Dr. Godbold attained national
prominence for his efforts on behalf of "inner city" community
colleges for his leadership in the establishment of the Council on
Black American Affairs (CBAA), and the establishment of National
Council on Black American Affairs (NCBAA). Dr. Godbold was the
first African American selected for a council seat on the Board of
Directors of the American Association of Junior Colleges. Dr.
Godbold has pioneered as the first African American in several
important educational administrative positions, most notably at the
Community College Level as a College Dean, President and CEO in
different states, Vice Chancellor, and the first African American
Chancellor of a multi-college/campus district in the state of
California. Dr. Godbold has written and published extensively about
the efficacy of Community College Education, especially as "second
chance" educational opportunities, particularly for those who have
had poor previous educational experiences, and minorities. The
President's Academy selected a speech he gave at an Education Policy
Conference held in Detroit, Michigan as one of the six best speeches

presented that was published for AAJC membership colleges. Dr. Godbold has "shepherded" and been a mentor for many "budding" community college professionals of all ethnicities who have aspired for educational careers in community college administration. Dr. Godbold has been an advocate for an Adjunct Individualized Self-Paced Instructional Methodology to benefit older students who seek educations at the Community College level, whose time management is a significant and important variable in their educational attainment.

GODBOLD.

"Believe that you can." –Godbold

www.ingramcontent.com/pod-product-compliance
Lightning Source LLC
Chambersburg PA
CBHW031516270326
41930CB00006B/424